scapino!

scapino!

**Adapted by Frank Dunlop and Jim Dale
from Molière's Comedy
"Les Fourberies de Scapin"**

Nelson Doubleday, Inc. Garden City, New York

The original American production of SCAPINO!
opened at the Circle-in-the-Square theatre in New
York on May 18, 1974. It was moved to the Am-
bassador Theatre on Broadway on September 27
of the same year.

Produced by Eugene V. Wolsk and Emanuel
  Azenberg
Directed by Frank Dunlop
Scenery and Costumes by Carl Toms
Music by Jim Dale
Lighting by Tharon Musser

CHARACTERS

OTTAVIO . . *son of the wealthy merchant, Argante*

SYLVESTRO . . . . *Ottavio's guardian*

SCAPINO . . *friend of Sylvestro, Leandro's guardian*

GIACINTA . . . . *in love with Ottavio*

ARGANTE . . . . *father of Ottavio*

GERONTE . . . . *father of Leandro*

LEANDRO . . . . . *friend of Ottavio, son of Geronte*

CARLO . . . . *a bum*

ZERBINETTA . . . . *a gypsy*

NURSE . . . . *of Giacinta*

HEADWAITER

TWO HARASSED WAITERS (One singing)

ONE WAITRESS (Lives in cafe)

TIME: *The present.*

PLACE: *The seaport of Naples, a cafe bar at the side of the dock.*

ORIGINAL NEW YORK CAST
(*in order of appearance*)

Scapino (servant of Geronte) . . . . JIM DALE

Headwaiter . . . . HUGH HASTINGS

Waiter . . . . ALAN COATES

Waitress . . . . JENNY AUSTEN

Carlo . . . . RAYMOND PLATT

Ottavio (son of Argante) . . . . . . CHRISTOPHER HASTINGS

Sylvestro (servant of Argante, friend to Scapino) . . GAVIN REED

Giacinta (beloved of Ottavio) . . . . TAMMY USTINOV

Argante . . . . IAN TRIGGER

Geronte . . . . PAUL BROOKE

Leandro (son of Geronte) . . . . . . JEREMY JAMES-TAYLOR

Zerbinetta (a gypsy, beloved of Leandro) . . . CLEO SYLVESTRE

Nurse . . . . LOTTI TAYLOR

scapino!

THE SETTING

No house curtain is used. The stage is preset and the curtain opened fifteen minutes before the show begins.

The setting of the play is a dockside cafe in Naples, and the main elements on stage are the cafe with its balconies on the left and right, a sidewalk, ramps, and a jetty (the forestage). Upstage of the jetty is a bit of the (imaginary) sea, where the boat is located. The sea is the Bay of Naples. The water on stage is not real—it is represented by a blue ground-cloth. The boat is real, however, as are the gaudy decorations.

GENERAL PROPERTIES

Three round tables (one with an umbrella), each with two or three chairs; a jukebox with records, a bench, small rowboat, coil of rope, garbage can, broom (with rubber crutch tip on handle) in the boat; a rope hanging down the left side of the right balcony; a large barrel. Also assorted crates, barrels, boxes, baskets, cans. When the play opens there are three tablecloths hung over the left balcony railing.

part one

(WAITRESS enters from cafe, yawning; puts five coins in jukebox, and selects songs. Jukebox does not begin so she kicks and slaps it. Music begins on slap. WAITRESS does warm-up exercises to music and exits into cafe. CARLO enters theatre from stage left and talks to audience in mock Italian. He climbs over barrels and boxes and starts to cross the stage. WAITRESS enters cafe balcony and picks up three tablecloths from railing. CARLO and WAITRESS on balcony exchange nasty glances. Seagulls are heard. WAITRESS exits as CARLO enters audience from stairs at rear of stage, talking to audience in mock Italian. Guitar solo of song "Minestrone Macaroni" is heard from inside cafe. Three WAITERS enter from cafe, jukebox stops, first hummed measures of "Minestrone Macaroni" are heard. HEADWAITER supervises the setting up of three tables—at left, center and right of stage. WAITER 1 crosses to right table, places broom against table, crosses to center table and sets chairs. WAITER 2 crosses to left table, sets chairs, and sweeps area in front of cafe. SCAPINO enters cafe balcony playing second measure of "Minestrone Macaroni." Seagulls fade. WAITRESS enters with tablecloths from cafe. She crosses to left table and leaves tablecloth. SCAPINO, on cafe balcony, and backstage singers begin singing "Minestrone Macaroni." They continue singing during the ensuing action.

MINESTRONE MACARONI

Pollo All Americana,
Scampi Fritti in Brodo
Pasta Bolognese,
Pate Mayonnaise,
Capuchino Espresso

Minestrone Macaroni,
Ravioli Aux Crevette,
Caramella In Padella,
Avocado Vinaigrette.

Scallopina Valdostana
Bistecca Con Risotto,
Pasta Bolognese
Pate Mayonnaise
Da Un Buon Appetito.

Minestrone Macaroni,
Ravioli Aux Crevette,
Caramella In Padella,
Avocado Vinaigrette.

WAITRESS crosses to right table and leaves tablecloth.
WAITER 1 finishes setting chairs at center table. He starts
to get broom, sees CARLO entering from right and chases
him into audience, yelling in mock Italian. WAITRESS
shakes out third tablecloth, crosses to center table as
WAITER 1 crosses to right table, passing her on bridge. He
fixes chairs and begins sweeping stage. WAITRESS places
tablecloth on center table. CARLO enters stage, sits at
center table and pinches her bottom. At first she doesn't
react, then as he persists she slaps him and begins to cross

upstage. CARLO pulls tablecloth over him like a blanket and goes to sleep. WAITRESS sees him, screams at him in mock Italian, grabs tablecloth, pulls him out of chair and throws him down stairs. He yells at her in mock Italian and then begins talking to audience. WAITRESS fixes tablecloth at table, crosses to right table and, with back to audience, fixes tablecloth. CARLO sneaks up behind her, looks up her skirt, looks to audience and looks up her skirt again. WAITRESS starts to cross to left. CARLO climbs on mainstage and exits. WAITER 1 throws broom to HEADWAITER, goes down on knee and makes a pass at WAITRESS as she pushes him out of her way. At this point, lyrics end, and melody of "Minestrone Macaroni" is hummed.

HEADWAITER throws his broom to WAITER 2 and makes a pass at WAITRESS as she pushes him out of the way. As WAITRESS crosses toward left table, WAITER 2 throws both brooms to HEADWAITER and falls on his knee and makes pass at WAITRESS. She slaps his face, straightens tablecloth, and exits. HEADWAITER throws both brooms to WAITER 1 and all WAITERS cross to exit into cafe. HEADWAITER exits through cafe doors, and bicycle horn is heard offstage. WAITER 1 and WAITER 2 see CARLO approaching cafe on a bicycle. They run to cafe and open doors as CARLO rides through doors and into cafe, followed by the WAITERS. A loud crash is heard from inside cafe followed by much hubbub and confusion.

CARLO is thrown out of cafe by the seat of his pants and back of his neck by WAITER 1. WAITER 1 reenters cafe as WAITER 2 exits cafe and throws a bicycle wheel at CARLO. WAITER 2 enters cafe as WAITER 1 exits cafe and throws handlebars at CARLO. WAITER 1 enters cafe as WAITER 2 exits cafe and throws bicycle seat at

CARLO. WAITER 2 enters cafe as WAITER 1 throws
SYLVESTRO out of cafe, who then falls on his knees next
to CARLO. CARLO whispers to SYLVESTRO as
WAITER 1 enters cafe. SYLVESTRO stands and runs to
meet OTTAVIO, who has entered from the right aisle and
is mounting the steps to the forestage. SYLVESTRO grabs
him and says, "Your father is back." Meanwhile CARLO
has picked up the three bicycle parts and exits. Yelling an
Italian expletive, OTTAVIO runs on stage and turns.)

OTTAVIO.   I'm lost, I'm ruined, what am I to do? Sad news to
an enamored heart! My world is crumbling around me.
Disaster after disaster. You've just heard, Sylvestro, that my
father is back.

SYLVESTRO.   Your father is back.

OTTAVIO.   His boat docked this very morning.

SYLVESTRO (sitting at center table).   This very morning.

OTTAVIO.   And that he's come back determined to marry me
off.

SYLVESTRO.   To marry you off.

OTTAVIO.   To a daughter of Signor Geronte.

SYLVESTRO.   Of Signore Geronte.

OTTAVIO.   And the daughter is already on her way back
from Marseilles to do the deed.

SYLVESTRO.   To do the deed.

OTTAVIO.   And this news was sent by my uncle.

SYLVESTRO.   By your uncle.

OTTAVIO (crossing below SYLVESTRO toward left
chair).   To whom my father sent it in a letter.

SYLVESTRO.   In a letter.

OTTAVIO.   And my uncle knows all we've been up to.

SYLVESTRO.   All we've been up to.

OTTAVIO (placing hat on table and sitting).   Oh, for
heaven's sake, say something instead of parroting
everything I say. (Hits table.)

SYLVESTRO.   Parroting every—(Hits hat instead of
    table.)—what more can I say? (Fixing hat.) You've
    remembered everything, spot on.
OTTAVIO.   Well, at least give me some advice. Tell me how I
    can get out of this terrible mess.
SYLVESTRO (an Italian expletive: "Oi Mama Leone").   I'm
    just as much in the mess as you are. I could do with a bit of
    advice myself.
OTTAVIO.   I'm ruined by this rotten return.
SYLVESTRO.   The ruin's mutual.
OTTAVIO (standing).   When my father finds out, I can see a
    thunderstorm of violent recriminations pouring on me.
    (SCAPINO exits cafe balcony.)
SYLVESTRO.   Recriminations pouring are nothing. It's me
    what'll have to suffer most. I can see a thunderstorm of
    belts on the ear bursting on me.
OTTAVIO.   Oh, God, how can I get out of this terrible mess!
SYLVESTRO.   You should have thought of that before you
    got into it.
OTTAVIO (crossing bridge).   It's not the time now to say "I
    told you so." What can I do? (Now he jumps across the
    water to SYLVESTRO.)
SYLVESTRO.   I don't know.
OTTAVIO.   What can I do? What can I do? (Grabs
    SYLVESTRO by neck and nearly pushes him into sea.)
SYLVESTRO.   I can't swim.

(Enter SCAPINO from cafe.)

SCAPINO.   How now, Signor Ottavio?
SYLVESTRO (pulling away from OTTAVIO).   Scapino!
SCAPINO (crossing toward bridge).   Hey! Hey! What's the
    matter? What's wrong with you? Something seems to be
    wrong . . . you look a little disturbed.

OTTAVIO (crossing bridge).   Oh, my dear Scapino, I'm
    ruined. I'm going mad. I'm the unhappiest man in the whole
    world.
SCAPINO.   Really? How's that?
OTTAVIO.   You mean to say you haven't heard what's
    happened to me?
SCAPINO.   No.
OTTAVIO (grabbing him by sleeve).   My father and Signor
    Geronte are back, and they're determined to marry me off.
SCAPINO.   Well, what's so horrible in that?
OTTAVIO (clutching sleeve).   Oh, if only you knew the cause
    of my trouble.
SCAPINO.   There, there, just you tell me everything. You
    know I'm always willing to listen when a young fellow's in
    trouble.
OTTAVIO (pulling SCAPINO downstage).   Oh, Scapino, if
    you can devise any means to get me out of this terrible mess
    that I'm in—(Kneeling.)—I'll be indebted to you for the
    rest of my life.
SCAPINO.   Well, there's not much I can't do once I've set my
    mind on it. The good Lord has blessed me with quite a
    genius for clever ideas and inspired inventions, which the
    less talented, in their jealousies, call deceits and trickery.
    (Moves toward SYLVESTRO.) But without a shadow of a
    doubt, there's never been another fellow to measure up to
    me—(Lifting chocolate bar from SYLVESTRO's
    pocket.)—when it comes down to a little bit of fiddling or
    making a slight adjustment in a tight situation. Chocolate?
    (Offering chocolate to SYLVESTRO and then, going
    downstage, to audience.) There's no one with a better
    reputation at the job, but talent and hard work just aren't
    appreciated these days. (Goes up to chair earlier vacated by
    OTTAVIO.) Since my affairs got a little troubled, I've
    given the whole thing up.

OTTAVIO (on the bridge).   What affairs and what troubles,
Scapino?

SCAPINO.   Oh, I had a little contretemps with the law.

OTTAVIO.   With the law?

SCAPINO (sitting).   Yes, we didn't quite agree on a certain
matter.

SYLVESTRO.   They didn't quite agree. (Sits.)

SCAPINO.   You know they treated me very badly, and I was
so struck by the ingratitude of my fellow men I decided I
would never lift up another finger from that day on to help
anybody. But I'm always willing to listen.

OTTAVIO.   You know, Scapino, that two months ago Signor
Geronte and my father set sail together on a business trip in
which both their interests were concerned.

SCAPINO.   Quite.

OTTAVIO (moving toward table).   And that Leandro and
myself were left by our fathers, myself in the care of
Sylvestro—(Hitting SYLVESTRO on the back.)—and
Leandro under *your* supervision.

SCAPINO.   And I've done my job very conscientiously.

SYLVESTRO (standing).   So have I. . . .

OTTAVIO (pushing SYLVESTRO back into chair).   Some
time afterwards Leandro met a young gypsy girl and fell
madly in love with her.

SCAPINO (laughing).   Quite.

OTTAVIO (going back across the bridge).   As we're great
friends he took me straight away into his confidence and we
went together to see the girl. Well, I thought she was quite
pretty, but not as pretty as he thought I would. He spoke
about nothing but her, day in, day out; hardly a moment
went by that he didn't boast to me about her beauty, her
charm, her wit, her every word. In fact, he got quite
annoyed with me because I wasn't as lovesick as he was.

SCAPINO.   Look . . . look . . . look . . . I don't quite see
where all this is leading up to.

OTTAVIO (after a slight pause).   One day . . .

SCAPINO.   Ah!

OTTAVIO.   When I was going with him to visit his obsession, we heard in a little house on a bystreet, the sound of sobbing mixed with a great many tears. We asked what was going on.

SCAPINO.   Yes, well, you would, wouldn't you? (To audience.) You'd say "What was going on?" Wouldn't you?

OTTAVIO.   A woman passing by told us two foreign women lived there in terrible conditions.

SCAPINO.   Well, what next?

OTTAVIO (mimes dragging LEANDRO).   Curiosity made me drag Leandro to see what was the matter. (Goes to bench as he mimes entering room.) We went into a little room where we saw an old woman dying . . . (SCAPINO and SYLVESTRO "Ah.") . . . a nurse crying . . . (SCAPINO and SYLVESTRO "Ah.") . . . and a young girl dissolved in tears, the most beautiful, the most exquisite that was ever seen.

SCAPINO.   Ah-ha. Oi-oi.

OTTAVIO.   Any other girl would have looked wretched in the state she was, wearing nothing . . .

SCAPINO and SYLVESTRO (double take). Eh . . .

OTTAVIO.   . . . but rags, hair falling disheveled about her shoulders, but even in that state she glittered like a thousand stars. (SYLVESTRO gets up, starts across the bridge.)

SCAPINO.   Yes, I'm beginning to get the point, yessssss. . . .

OTTAVIO.   If you'd seen her, Scapino, in the state I had found her, you would have found her devastating.

SCAPINO.   I don't doubt it. And without seeing her I realize she must have that certain . . . (SYLVESTRO and SCAPINO: "Whoops.") . . . something. (SYLVESTRO has now crossed left and disappeared into the cafe.)

OTTAVIO.   Her tears weren't those ugly tears which make a

face red and swollen. She cried in the prettiest way
imaginable, and her misery was the most beautiful misery in
the world.

SCAPINO. Yes. . . . Obviously.

(SYLVESTRO comes from the cafe with two Cokes and glasses
and returns to the table as OTTAVIO continues.)

OTTAVIO. Sobbing . . . (Kneels.) . . . she threw herself on
her knees beside the dying woman, and called her
"Mother."

SYLVESTRO. Eh. (Stopping momentarily by OTTAVIO.)

OTTAVIO. Everyone felt tears come into their eyes to see
such love and affection. (SYLVESTRO, now at table, turns
bottles over into glasses.)

SCAPINO. Very moving indeed, and I suppose that one lot of
love and affection sort of gave birth to another.

OTTAVIO. Scapino, a *stone* wall would have loved her.

SCAPINO. Quite.

(SYLVESTRO, realizing the Coke bottles are unopened, runs
and hands them to OTTAVIO and runs back to SCAPINO.
In frustration, OTTAVIO tries to take bottle top off with
his teeth and then with his shoe. He then uses Coke bottles
as binoculars. He looks to cafe and slowly turns right,
looking through "binoculars." CARLO enters from right,
walks to OTTAVIO, observing the activity, and stops in
front of him as OTTAVIO sees CARLO through
"binoculars." CARLO takes bottle opener from pocket,
shows it to OTTAVIO, who gives him one of the bottles.
CARLO opens the bottle, puts top in OTTAVIO's hand
[OTTAVIO is listening to SYLVESTRO] and begins
exit toward cafe. OTTAVIO extends his bottle for a toast,
CARLO stops, clinks bottles and exits through cafe

drinking Coke. OTTAVIO tries to drink his Coke and
realizes the cap is still on.)

SYLVESTRO.   Now look, if you don't cut the story short we'll
  be listening here till tomorrow. Now I'll finish it in two
  words. His heart burst into flames. He couldn't live without
  the girl. He's never off the doorstep. His visits to comfort
  the unhappy girl make him more of a lodger than a visitor.
  The nurse forbids him the house. Irresistible force.
  (SYLVESTRO and SCAPINO: "Immovable object.") He
  begs, he grovels, he argues. Not a hope. For though the girl
  is without money and friends, she comes from a good
  family, and unless he marries her, he's got to keep his hands
  off her. (SYLVESTRO moves right, then up across the
  bridge, turning back again as he continues his speech.)
  Passion feeds on obstacles. He wracks his brain, ponders,
  reasons, debates and then makes up his mind, and he's been
  a married man for the last three days. Now add to that the
  unexpected return of his father; add to that the other
  marriage his father's arranged with Signor Geronte's
  daughter, that's the daughter of a second wife Geronte
  married at Marseilles. (OTTAVIO comes beside
  SYLVESTRO, who is now standing on the bridge.)
OTTAVIO (handing Coke back to SYLVESTRO).   And
  worse than all this, add the poverty in which my poor,
  lovely wife now lives and my inability, penniless as I am, to
  help her. (Sits on rope.)
SYLVESTRO.   There.
SCAPINO (standing, crossing to OTTAVIO).   Is that all? Do
  you know the pair of you seem bowled over by nothing. I
  mean, what on earth are you worried for? (Goes up on
  bridge.) Aren't you ashamed to be panicked by such a little
  thing? What the devil, you've been to the Actor's Studio,
  and you can't stir your brain to some little stratagem, some
  little wheeze to put things right. (Now in front of bench.)

Do you know I was no bigger than that, when I was clearing up matters a thousand times more complicated. Oh, if only my legal mix-up had not made me swear off such temptation.

SYLVESTRO (moving to right end of bench as SCAPINO moves to left end). Yes, well, I realize I haven't been blessed with your brains.

SCAPINO. That's true, very true.

SYLVESTRO. And that I haven't got your genius . . .

(GIACINTA enters top of right aisle.)

SYLVESTRO. . . . for getting mixed up with the law, but . . .

GIACINTA (seeing OTTAVIO and running toward him). Ottavio!

OTTAVIO (going to her). Here comes my lovely Giacinta.

GIACINTA. Ottavio! (They meet at the lower end of the bridge. GIACINTA kisses OTTAVIO and kneels. SCAPINO and SYLVESTRO sit on bench and watch.) Oh, Ottavio, is it true what Sylvestro told Nerina? Your father's back and is going to marry you to someone else? (With tears in her eyes.)

OTTAVIO. Yes, my dearest, and I'm as heartbroken as you are. But—(Kneeling.)—what's this? You're crying. Why these tears? Surely you don't suspect that I'll be unfaithful to you? Surely you don't doubt my love for you?

GIACINTA. Yes, Ottavio, I'm sure you love me, but I'm not so sure you'll always love me.

OTTAVIO. How could anyone love you without loving you for the rest of one's life?

GIACINTA. I've heard, Ottavio, that your sex loves not so long as ours does, and those burning passions men discover are as easily extinguished as they are set alight. (Turns to OTTAVIO.)

OTTAVIO.   My dear Giacinta, I'm not *made* like other men
. . .

SCAPINO and SYLVESTRO (crossing left legs over right).
Oh, my God!

OTTAVIO (crossing to GIACINTA).   . . . I know that I
shall love you till I die.

GIACINTA.   I'm sure you believe what you say, and don't
doubt that your words are sincere, but I fear a stronger
adversary than the tender feelings you have for me. You're
completely dependent on your father, who is determined to
marry you to someone else. If that happens I expect I'll die.
(She sits on bridge step and bursts into tears.)

OTTAVIO (kneeling and taking her hands).   No father shall
make me break my word to you. (SCAPINO and
SYLVESTRO cross to behind GIACINTA and
OTTAVIO, joking as if they are on a film set shooting a
love scene, SCAPINO miming camera and SYLVESTRO
using Coke bottle as microphone. They return to bench.
OTTAVIO and GIACINTA stand.) I would rather give up
my country, life itself, than give up you. Already without
having seen her I hate the girl he wishes me to marry. Don't
cry, dearest Giacinta, your tears hurt me more than you,
every one—(Kisses her eye.)—wounds me—(Kisses other
eye.)—to the heart. (Kisses her lips.)

GIACINTA (crossing stage).   To make you happy, I shall
hold back my tears, and wait with dry eyes for whatever
Fate has in store.

OTTAVIO (crossing to GIACINTA).   Fate is on our side.

GIACINTA.   It must be, if you stay true to me.

OTTAVIO.   Never doubt that.

GIACINTA.   Then I *shall* be happy. (They hug.)

SCAPINO (to SYLVESTRO).   She's not such a fool—eh!
(Stands.) She's quite nice to look at, too. (SCAPINO
begins to exit right.) Ciao!

OTTAVIO (turning and running after SCAPINO). Here's a
man who could be a marvelous help to us if he were willing.

SCAPINO (stopping and turning to OTTAVIO and
GIACINTA). Now, you know I've resolved never to
meddle in anyone else's business again—no . . . but . . .
(Staring at GIACINTA.) . . . if you were both to ask me
very nicely . . . perhaps . . .

OTTAVIO. Oh, if it's only a question of asking nicely, my
dearest Scapino—(Going on his knees.) I beg you with all
my heart to be the captain of our ship.

SCAPINO (still staring at GIACINTA, then turning to
OTTAVIO). Pardon . . . Ah, yes. (Crosses down and
pats OTTAVIO's head and says to GIACINTA.) And you,
have you nothing to say to me? (SCAPINO wipes hand.)

GIACINTA (crossing to SCAPINO). I beg you by everything
that's dear to you to help us and our love. (She grabs his
tie, pulls him to her in three moves and kisses him.)

SCAPINO (after kiss). Right, I've been argued 'round. You
get along, then; I'll do some thinking on your behalf.
(GIACINTA starts to exit. SYLVESTRO crosses to cafe
and puts Coke on barrel by cafe door.)

OTTAVIO. Believe me, I . . .

SCAPINO. Chut! (To GIACINTA.) Just get along home and
stop worrying. Ciao!

GIACINTA (exiting, turning at foot of stairs). Ciao!

SCAPINO. Ciao!

GIACINTA (still exiting). Ciao!

SCAPINO (to SYLVESTRO). What a lovely girl. Ciao!

GIACINTA (exiting stage left aisle). Ciao! (SCAPINO
throws her a kiss.)

SCAPINO (to OTTAVIO). Ah, yes . . . you get your upper
lip stiffened to meet your father.

OTTAVIO (crossing to chair at right table, and sitting). I
must admit my lip's trembling already. I suffer from a sort
of natural cowardice that I just can't overcome.

SCAPINO.   You must seem master from the moment you
    meet, or he'll take advantage of your weakness and treat
    you like a child. You must learn to look com—com—
    com—(To SYLVESTRO, who has crossed back to
    SCAPINO.) What's the word? . . . Com—
SYLVESTRO.   . . . um . . . compost.
SCAPINO.   Composed. A little boldness, and answer him
    firmly whatever he says.

(CARLO enters from cafe drinking glass of Coke.
    SYLVESTRO meets him at bench and takes Coke.
    CARLO takes Coke bottle from pocket and drinks. The
    others watch.)

OTTAVIO.   I'll do the best I can. (He stands.)
SCAPINO.   Right. We could have a little rehearsal here to get
    you used to it. We have the audience here. We'll play the
    scene together and see how well you'll act it. Now, don't
    forget. Mind resolute, head high, firm looks.
OTTAVIO (taking pose).   Like this?
SCAPINO.   Come on. . . . Firm looks, head high, chin out.
OTTAVIO.   O.K. now?
SCAPINO.   Yes, that's all right. Now imagine I'm your father
    just arrived and answer me firmly as if I were him. I'm
    coming on now. (Imitating ARGANTE.) "Who ever heard
    of such a thing? What an idiot thing to do. (CARLO and
    SYLVESTRO choke on their Cokes and spit them into
    sea.) Ah, there you are worthless, notorious—(Crossing
    right.)—son, unworthy of a father like me. How dare you
    stand before me after this fine behavior, this cheap trick
    you've played whilst I've been away. Is this the fruit of all
    my toils, lout? (He has now reached OTTAVIO.) The
    respect you owe me, the respect you owe me for my care of
    you?" Say something! (OTTAVIO tries to say something
    but SCAPINO stops him.) "You have the cheek, you

beetle, to get married without your father's consent—to marry secretly without even his knowledge? Answer me, you lout, answer me. Give me one good reason."
(OTTAVIO tries to say something again with arm and forefinger extended. He fails, his finger, then arm, slowly collapsing.)

OTTAVIO.   It's because you sound exactly like my father.

SCAPINO.   Well, of course I do. That's why you mustn't act like an idiot.

OTTAVIO.   I'll do better this time. I'll be firm and . . . (Gulp.) . . . determined.

SCAPINO.   Determined?

OTTAVIO.   Determined.

SCAPINO.   Definitely?

OTTAVIO.   Definitely.

SYLVESTRO.   Good. Here comes your father now.

(ARGANTE growls from lobby, then runs down left house aisle to forestage.)

OTTAVIO.   Oh, God, I'm lost. (He rushes off right. CARLO leaves through cafe and SYLVESTRO crosses into cafe, coming out on balcony.)

SCAPINO.   Hey there, Ottavio, hold on a minute. Quite a turn of speed! What a weak-kneed specimen. Well, Sylvestro, we'll have to deal with the old man ourselves.

SYLVESTRO (on balcony).   What shall I tell him?

SCAPINO.   Well . . . agree with me and back me up. (Exits cafe. ARGANTE, speaking to himself, is now on forestage.)

ARGANTE.   Who ever heard of such a thing. (Bangs table with cane and crosses to right table.)

(HEADWAITER enters, crosses to table and mimes taking order from ARGANTE.)

SYLVESTRO.   He's already heard about it, and he's so furious
    that he's having a row with himself about it.
ARGANTE.   What a lunatic thing to do. (Bangs table.)

(SCAPINO enters cafe balcony.)

SCAPINO.   Let's listen awhile.
ARGANTE.   I'd love to know what they dare to say to me
    about this damned marriage. (Bangs table.
    HEADWAITER checks off appetizer on menu.)
SCAPINO.   We're just thinking about it.
ARGANTE.   Will they try to deny it?
SCAPINO.   No, I don't think we'll do that.
ARGANTE.   Or will they try to make excuses?
SCAPINO.   That's possible.
ARGANTE.   Perhaps they'll try to entertain me with fairy
    stories. (Bangs table. HEADWAITER checks off entree.)
SCAPINO.   Perhaps. Eh?
ARGANTE.   Everything they say will be useless. (Bangs table.
    HEADWAITER checks off dessert and exits to cafe.)
SCAPINO.   We'll see about that.
ARGANTE.   They shan't make an idiot of me.
SCAPINO.   Ho ho. Don't you count on it.
ARGANTE.   I'll make sure that rascal of a son of mine is kept
    safe.
SCAPINO.   And we've the same intention.
ARGANTE.   And as for that ferret Sylvestro, I'll . . . I'll . . .
    I'll . . . beat him to a jelly.
SYLVESTRO.   I knew he'd remember me. (SCAPINO and
    SYLVESTRO do hand-slapping game. Seeing
    SYLVESTRO on balcony and SCAPINO leaving balcony,
    ARGANTE runs to cafe.)
ARGANTE.   Ah-ha. So you're there, are you? (Jumps under
    balcony and hits balcony with cane, causing SYLVESTRO
    to jump.) Wise custodian of a family—(ARGANTE hits

balcony and SYLVESTRO jumps.)—fine director of
morals of the young. (ARGANTE hits balcony and
SYLVESTRO jumps.)

(SCAPINO enters from cafe and takes ARGANTE by the arm,
drawing him toward center stage.)

SCAPINO. Sir, I am ravished to see you home again.
ARGANTE. How do, Scapino. (Breaks away from SCAPINO
and goes back to under balcony. To SYLVESTRO.)
You've carried out my orders very prettily, haven't you?
(Hits balcony and SYLVESTRO jumps.)
SYLVESTRO. I've done my best.
ARGANTE. My son's behaved himself only too well whilst
I've been away. (Hits balcony and SYLVESTRO jumps.)
SCAPINO (taking ARGANTE by the arm again). You're
looking very well as far as I can see.
ARGANTE. Glowing. (Breaking away from SCAPINO and
saying to SYLVESTRO.) Well, can't you say anything,
idiot? (Hits balcony and SYLVESTRO jumps.) Can't you
say anything? (Hits balcony and SYLVESTRO jumps.)
SCAPINO (taking ARGANTE by arm again and crossing to
right). Did you have a pleasant journey back, sir?
(SYLVESTRO exits balcony.)
ARGANTE (breaking away from SCAPINO as they near the
bench at center). Very pleasant, and for God's sake, leave
me alone and let me have a row in peace.
SCAPINO (following, as ARGANTE continues right). You
want a row?
ARGANTE. Yes, I want a row.
SCAPINO. With whom, sir?

(SYLVESTRO enters from cafe. ARGANTE points to him
with his cane.)

ARGANTE.   With that streak there. (During the ensuing
   dialogue, SYLVESTRO unobtrusively moves to sit on the
   bridge by going down the steps left, by the boat, then down
   again, and crossing below forestage to right and up onto the
   bridge without using the steps. He listens to the
   conversation.)
SCAPINO.   And why?
ARGANTE.   You've not heard what's gone on whilst I've been
   away?
SCAPINO.   Well . . . well . . . I did hear a few little jokey
   things, sir.
ARGANTE (crossing to table on forestage).   A few little
   jokey things! A catastrophe like this?
SCAPINO (following to bridge).   Maybe you see things a little
   differently.
ARGANTE.   An astounding piece of insolence like this.
SCAPINO.   Weeeeeeeelllllllll . . .
ARGANTE (sitting at table).   A son to get married without
   the consent of his father.

(WAITER 1 enters, crosses to center table and places napkin,
   spoon and fork.)

SCAPINO.   Yes, I know, it is very unusual. But I don't think
   you should make too much fuss about it.
ARGANTE.   Well, I *do* think I should. (WAITER 1 finishes
   setting table and exits.) And I'll have my bellyful of making
   a fuss about it. Don't you think I've got every reason in the
   world to be furious?

(HEADWAITER enters from cafe, crosses to center stage and
   checks off dishes on order pad as they are brought on and
   handed to SCAPINO, who places them in front of
   ARGANTE.)

SCAPINO. Quite. (Puts napkin around ARGANTE.)

(CARLO enters house and makes his way to stage.)

SCAPINO. I was just the same myself, sir, just after I heard the news.

(WAITER 2 enters with bread and crosses to SCAPINO.)

SCAPINO. . . . and I was so incensed on your behalf I had an enormous row with your son.

(WAITER 1 enters carrying spaghetti.)

SCAPINO. You just ask him how I shouted . . .

(SCAPINO takes break from WAITER 2, who crosses to take wine from WAITRESS [who enters from cafe] to give to SCAPINO.)

SCAPINO. . . . how I lectured to him on the respect he owed a father whose footsteps he's not good enough to kiss. (CARLO, on stage, prepares to shine ARGANTE's shoes.) You couldn't have done better yourself, sir, but what good does it do? I sat down and I thought and I reasoned—(Taking wine.)—out that at the bottom of it all he might not be so much in the wrong as one might think. (All WAITERS and WAITRESS exit. CARLO puts ARGANTE's foot on shoebox. SCAPINO sits and pours wine.)
ARGANTE (pulling foot away from CARLO). What kind of clever double-talk is this? There's nothing wrong in getting married—point-blank—to a stranger?
SCAPINO. Yes, but . . . what would you have him do? Fate

led him to it. (CARLO takes ARGANTE's foot again and
shines his shoe. SCAPINO hands ARGANTE a glass of
wine and takes one for himself.)

ARGANTE.   Oh-ho, the easiest excuse in the world. One's
only to commit the worst crimes imaginable, cheat, steal,
murder and say for excuse, "Fate led me to it." (SCAPINO
begins readying spaghetti on fork.)

SCAPINO.   Oh, good Lord, sir, no . . . no . . . no. . . . You
take my words too literally. No, I meant to say that he
found himself fatally embroiled in this affair.

ARGANTE.   Why . . . (SCAPINO puts forkful of spaghetti
in ARGANTE's mouth. Audience laughs. CARLO spits in
shoeshine rag. ARGANTE reacts with a mouthful of
spaghetti.) Why did he become fatally embroiled?

SCAPINO (readying more spaghetti).   Now surely, sir, you
can't expect him to have the intelligence that you have?
Young folks are . . .

ARGANTE.   Young . . . (More spaghetti in ARGANTE's
mouth.)

SCAPINO (breaking off a piece of roll).   Exactly. And haven't
the intelligence to keep them on the straight and narrow,
doing nothing but what's reasonable. Now take our
Leandro, for example . . .

ARGANTE (having chewed spaghetti).   Oh! . . .

SCAPINO (putting bread in ARGANTE's mouth).   . . . in
spite of all I've taught him, in spite of all my remonstrances,
has gone and done worse than your son.

ARGANTE.   Worse than my son?

SCAPINO (nodding his head).   Yes!

ARGANTE.   He has? Tell me more. (CARLO stops shining
shoes and listens.)

SCAPINO.   Now, weren't you young once yourself, and didn't
you once sow the odd wild oat? I've heard that you were
quite a one for the signorinas in your day, and when you

made an attack you never withdrew till the defenses were
down.

ARGANTE (laughing, with mouthful of food).   Yes, that's
true. I don't know who the devil told you, but it's very true.

ARGANTE and SCAPINO (to each other).   It's very true.
(To the audience.) It's very true. (To the audience with
CARLO.) It's very true.

ARGANTE.   You've made a point there. But I never got
myself into the fix he's done.

SCAPINO (standing).   What would you have him do? He sees
a young lady who shows an affection for him, for he takes
after you to have all the women in love with him. (CARLO
getting chummy with ARGANTE.)

ARGANTE.   Yes, yes, yes, I know.

SCAPINO (moving to bridge).   He finds her enchanting. He
pays her visits, murmurs sweet nothings, sighs with passion.
She lets herself be caught, he pushes his luck. Whoops!
Surprised with her by her parents he's manhandled to the
church where he is forced at gunpoint to marry her.

SYLVESTRO (standing).   How does he do it?

SCAPINO (to ARGANTE, moving back to table).   Look,
would you have had him let himself be killed, sir? It's a far,
far better thing to be married than to be dead. (CARLO
stands up, claps and says "Bravo.")

ARGANTE (standing).   They didn't tell me it had
happened quite like that.

SCAPINO.   Well, just you ask him, sir. He'll give you the same
answer. (ARGANTE crosses to SYLVESTRO. CARLO
sits in ARGANTE's chair and eats crumbs from bread
basket.)

ARGANTE.   Was it by force that he was married?

SYLVESTRO.   No—yes, signor.

SCAPINO (who has followed ARGANTE).   Would I tell you
a lie, sir?

ARGANTE.   Well, then he should have gone straight to the
    police and reported the assault.
SCAPINO.   That's just what he couldn't do.
ARGANTE.   It would have made it much easier for me to
    dissolve the marriage.
SCAPINO.   Dissolve the marriage?
ARGANTE.   Yes.
SCAPINO.   You wouldn't dissolve it.
ARGANTE.   I wouldn't dissolve it?
SCAPINO.   No!
ARGANTE.   No?
SCAPINO.   No!
ARGANTE.   No?
SCAPINO.   No!
ARGANTE.   No?
SYLVESTRO.   No! (Runs away, over the bridge to stage
    right.)
ARGANTE.   What? (Crossing upstage.) Why shouldn't I
    have the rights of a father? And have satisfaction for the
    violence they've used against my son?
SCAPINO (following him upstage, then going to bench).   It's
    something he won't really agree with.
ARGANTE.   He won't really agree with?
SCAPINO.   No.
ARGANTE.   My son?   (Goes to SCAPINO.)
SCAPINO (face to face with ARGANTE).   Your son! Do you
    want him to have to confess publicly that he was frightened
    to death and that he was such a coward as to let himself be
    forced to marry her? He'd never be able to look anyone else
    in the face again. He'd feel himself unworthy of a father
    like you.
ARGANTE.   That's a joke.
SCAPINO.   No, look, he must for his honor and yours let
    everyone think he married her of his own free will.
ARGANTE (nose to nose with SCAPINO as text goes

faster). And I must, for my honor and for his, prove the contrary.

SCAPINO. No. I don't think he'll do it.

ARGANTE. I'll force him to.

SCAPINO. He won't do it, I'm certain of it.

ARGANTE. He will do it, or I'll disinherit him.

SCAPINO. You?

ARGANTE. Me.

SCAPINO. Good.

ARGANTE. What do you mean, good?

SCAPINO. You won't disinherit him.

ARGANTE. I won't disinherit him?

SCAPINO. No.

ARGANTE. No?

SCAPINO. No.

ARGANTE. Very funny. I won't disinherit my son.

SCAPINO. No.

ARGANTE. And who is going to stop me?

SCAPINO. You will.

ARGANTE. Me?

SCAPINO. Yes, you. You won't have the heart to do it.

ARGANTE. I will.

SCAPINO. You're joking.

ARGANTE. I am *not* joking.

SCAPINO. Fatherly tenderness will prevail.

ARGANTE. Oh, no, it won't.

SCAPINO. Oh, yes, it will.

ARGANTE. I tell you, it shall be done.

SCAPINO (imitating ARGANTE). Oh . . . fff . . . fiddle-de-dee.

ARGANTE. Don't say "ff . . . fiddle-de-dee" to me.

SCAPINO. Now come on, sir, you're naturally too good-natured.

ARGANTE. I am not good-natured, not at all good-natured.

SYLVESTRO (crossing downstage, to audience). . . . He's
     not good-natured, not at all good-natured.
ARGANTE. . . . and I can be the very devil when I want to
     be. (Moves right.)
SCAPINO (to audience). . . . oh, he is, too. Second act, he's
     fantastic.
ARGANTE. Let's have no more of this silly chitchat or I'll
     burst. (To SYLVESTRO.) Get out, pearshape. Go and
     find that rascal of a son of mine whilst I go join Signor
     Geronte to tell him of the scandal. (SYLVESTRO runs
     down the steps and out.)
SCAPINO. Sir, if I can be of any help at any time, just you
     send for me. Call, and I shall be at your service.
ARGANTE. Thank you. (To himself.) Oh, why should
     Ottavio be an only child? If only my daughter had been
     spared to me I'd have left all my money to her. (Exits
     right. CARLO puts away brush, rag and polish and runs
     after ARGANTE.)
CARLO. Momento, Signore . . . Signore, momento. (Stops
     near SCAPINO.) . . . shoeshine, signore?
SCAPINO. Suede, you're joking. (CARLO exits right.)

(SYLVESTRO, meanwhile, has mounted the steps to the
     forestage and crossed right to SCAPINO. HEADWAITER
     enters with bill on plate and crosses to SCAPINO.)

SYLVESTRO. I agree, you're a genius, and you've done
     marvelously well so far, but there's the matter of money.
SCAPINO (taking plate from HEADWAITER). Money?
     (Gives plate to SYLVESTRO and crosses to center table,
     pours wine and sits. SYLVESTRO puts lire on plate and
     gives it to HEADWAITER.)
SYLVESTRO (crossing to center table and sitting). Money.
     There's not only eating to consider, but the creditors are

beginning to chase me down the street. (HEADWAITER
takes lire, puts change on plate and crosses to table.)

SCAPINO. Leave it to me. The plot is hatched.
(HEADWAITER at table offers change. SYLVESTRO
takes it and begins to put it in his pocket. SCAPINO snaps
his fingers, takes coin and puts it on the plate as a tip.
SYLVESTRO takes it again. HEADWAITER exits.)
At the moment I am trying to think of a man who I can
trust to play a part I need. (SCAPINO looks through
audience, then to SYLVESTRO who has been winding
spaghetti on his fork. SCAPINO grabs fork.) Hold it.
Make your hand into a fist. (SYLVESTRO does it.)
Put your hat on one side of your head. (SYLVESTRO
does so.) Stand up! (He does, and so does SCAPINO.)
Lean on one leg. (He does.) Put that hand into your pocket.
(He does.) Now make your eyes into slits. (He does.)
Good! That's it. Can you see?

SYLVESTRO. No.

SCAPINO. Now strut around like one of those gangsters in the
films we've been watching.

SYLVESTRO (strutting around). Like this?

SCAPINO. I think we've been watching the wrong films.
Come on. Like this! Oh, yes, yes. Now a couple-a more
disguises for your face and voice.

SYLVESTRO. Just as long as you don't get mixed up with the
law.

SCAPINO. What's ten years up the river when you're with a
friend?

SYLVESTRO. I can't swim.

(SYLVESTRO and SCAPINO begin to exit, going over the
bridge and across the upstage area toward the cafe, as the
HEADWAITER enters, goes down the left stairs and up
the stairs to the center table.)

SCAPINO.   Let's have a word with Godfather. (They exit
   upstage, beyond the cafe.)

The whole cast (offstage) sings as action continues.

POLLO ALL AMERICANA

Pollo All Americana,
Scampi Fritti in Brodo
Pasta Bolognese,
Pate Mayonnaise,
Capuchino Espresso

Minestrone Macaroni,
Ravioli Aux Crevette,
Caramella In Padella,
Avocado Vinaigrette.

Scallopina Valdostana
Bistecca Con Rissoto,
Pasta Bolognese
Pate Mayonnaise
Da Un Buon Appetito.

Minestrone Macaroni,
Ravioli Aux Crevette,
Caramella In Padella,
Avocado Vinaigrette.

(HEADWAITER takes spoon and fork off spaghetti plate and
   rolls them in a napkin he has brought on with him.
   WAITER 2 enters from cafe yawning and stretching. He
   crosses to right and takes a position on the bridge.

HEADWAITER takes fork and spoon in napkin and
puts it in breadbasket. CARLO enters from cafe and
leans against balcony post. HEADWAITER throws
basket to WAITER 2 who throws it to a suprised CARLO
who throws it through cafe doors where it is caught by
WAITER 1. They then throw the three rolls and the wine
carafe. HEADWAITER takes wine glasses, puts
them on chair, and with great flair pulls tablecloth out from
under spaghetti plate. He throws tablecloth to WAITER 2,
who puts it over his arm. HEADWAITER then picks up
spaghetti plate, holds it to audience as the singing in cafe
stops. He makes three turns to audience with plate high in
the air and then throws it to WAITER. He then sits on
stage steps and toasts himself with wine glass. WAITER 2
throws plate to CARLO who barely catches it and then
throws it into cafe where we hear it crash. After crash,
singing begins again. WAITERS and CARLO exit quickly
into cafe. Singing stops after they exit. Enter GERONTE
and ARGANTE from right. ARGANTE crosses to stage
left. GERONTE sits on bench.)

ARGANTE.   Who ever heard of such a thing. What a thing to
  do. I wonder what they have to say to me? . . . etc. . . .
  etc.
GERONTE (hitting umbrella on floor).   What you have just
  told me about your son's scandalous behavior ruins the
  preparations we have made together.
ARGANTE (crossing to bench and sitting).   Now don't you
  worry yourself about that. I'll be responsible for the
  removal of that obstacle, and I'm going to see about it this
  very minute.
GERONTE.   Well, my goodness gracious me, Signor Argante,
  I really must say the education of children is a matter which
  demands a great deal of conscientious application.

ARGANTE.   Yes, that's very true. But why bring that up now?

GERONTE.   It has just occurred to me that the bad behavior
of young people usually springs from the bad education
their fathers give them.

ARGANTE.   Yes, I suppose so. . . . What exactly do you
mean by that?

GERONTE.   What exactly do I mean by that?

ARGANTE.   Yes.

GERONTE.   That if like a responsible father you had brought
up your son properly he would not have played this trick on
you.

ARGANTE.   Charming! And we can take it that you have
brought up your son without a flaw.

GERONTE.   Without a floor? Oh, without a flaw! No question
of it. And I should be very put out if my son had done
anything even approaching your son's behavior.

ARGANTE.   And, oh, what if this son of yours, brought up so
properly by his responsible father, had got into a worse
mess than mine? Eh?

GERONTE.   Worse mess than . . . what do you mean?

ARGANTE.   What do I mean?

GERONTE.   What are you getting at?

ARGANTE.   What I'm getting at, Signor Geronte, is that we
shouldn't be so quick to criticize other people's behavior.
People who throw stones should make sure the windows are
boarded up at home.

GERONTE.   I'm not very good at riddles.

ARGANTE (standing).   Well, get someone to explain it to
you then.

GERONTE (stopping ARGANTE with umbrella).   You
wouldn't by any chance have heard a little something about
my son?

ARGANTE.   It's quite possible.

GERONTE (standing).   Well, spit it out then.

ARGANTE. Your fellow Scapino gave me the outline. In my own fury I missed the details, but I'm quite sure most of Naples can fill in those for you. (GERONTE sits.) Well, I am off to consult a lawyer, to find out what's best to do next. Arrivederci. (Exits left.)

GERONTE. Arrivederci. (Stands.) What can it be? A worse mess than his? I can't think of anything he could do worse.

(LEANDRO starts down house left aisle.)

GERONTE. Marrying without a father's consent is the worst thing I can think of.

LEANDRO (entering forestage, turning to look back). Ciao! (Throws a kiss.) Carissima. (He runs upstage, then sees his father and stops.)

GERONTE and LEANDRO (simultaneously). Ah-ha, there you are. (LEANDRO runs to embrace his father.)

LEANDRO. Father, what a delight to see you back in Naples.

GERONTE (refusing to embrace him, holding him off with umbrella). Take it easy. I've a little something to discuss with you first.

LEANDRO. But, Father, surely you'll let me embrace you.

GERONTE (holding him off with umbrella as it opens). Keep off, I tell you.

LEANDRO. But, surely, you'll let me show my happiness by my welcome.

GERONTE. Certainly, but first we have a little something to sort out together.

LEANDRO (crossing to left of GERONTE). Oh, and what may that be?

GERONTE. Hold still and let me look you straight in the eye.

LEANDRO (stopping and turning). But, Father . . .

GERONTE. Look me straight in the eye.

LEANDRO (taking sunglasses off and putting in pocket). Very well. (Stepping face-to-face with GERONTE.)

GERONTE.   What has been going on here?

LEANDRO.   Going on?

GERONTE.   Yes. What have you been doing while I've been away?

LEANDRO.   What would you have liked me to have done, Father?

GERONTE.   It's not a matter of what I might have liked you to have done, I'm asking you what it is you *have* done. (Hits LEANDRO on arm.)

LEANDRO (as both turn front).   I don't think I've done anything that would give you cause for concern.

GERONTE.   Nothing at all?

LEANDRO.   Nothing.

GERONTE.   You're very certain.

LEANDRO.   That's because I know I've done nothing wrong.

GERONTE.   Scapino seems to think otherwise.

LEANDRO.   Scapino?

GERONTE.   Ha, ha, ha. That makes you blush.

LEANDRO.   Did he tell you something about me?

GERONTE.   Did he tell me . . . this place is not very suitable to settle this business with all these people watching. We'll settle this at home. Go there immediately. (Hits LEANDRO's arm.) Don't talk to anyone on the way. (Hits LEANDRO's arm.) I'll be back myself in a moment. (Tries to hit LEANDRO again and misses. LEANDRO, moving away, almost falls into sea. GERONTE crosses down to front stage left.) You're a disgrace. If you've brought dishonor on the good name of Geronte, I'll throw you out and you'll never darken my door again. My door's quite dark enough as it is . . . (Exits down steps and up aisle.)

LEANDRO (now at forestage).   How could Scapino betray me like this? A weasel who for a hundred reasons ought to be the first to keep to himself my secrets is the first to give

me away to my father. I could tear him into a thousand
pieces and feed him to the fishes.

(Enter OTTAVIO and SCAPINO from cafe, the latter eating a
mock sausage.)

OTTAVIO.   Dear Scapino, I don't know how to thank you.
Heaven smiled on me when it sent you to my help.
LEANDRO (running up to SCAPINO).   Ah-ha, there you
are. What ecstasy to see you again, Master Trickster.
SCAPINO (bowing).   Oh, your servant, sir. Your servant. You
flatter me.
LEANDRO (grabbing sausage).   Don't make cruel jokes with
me.
SCAPINO.   Sir!
LEANDRO.   I'll teach you a lesson. (Tries to hit SCAPINO
with sausage. SCAPINO ducks and he hits OTTAVIO.
SCAPINO flees left, LEANDRO in pursuit. OTTAVIO
runs after them.)
OTTAVIO (trying to stop LEANDRO).   Leandro!
LEANDRO.   No, Ottavio, don't try to stop me, please.
SCAPINO.   But, sir . . .
OTTAVIO.   Calm yourself.
LEANDRO (trying to hit SCAPINO).   Just let me pay him
back.
OTTAVIO.   Leandro, don't be so violent.
SCAPINO.   What have I done, sir?
LEANDRO.   What have you done? Traitor. (Kicking
SCAPINO, who jumps into boat.)
OTTAVIO.   Take it easy.
LEANDRO (going down steps to boat).   No, Ottavio, I mean
to make him confess here and now the dirty trick he's
played. (Hits SCAPINO.) You scum, I know the game
you've been up to. You didn't expect the story would come

back to me so quickly. Come on, out with it, confess it was
your doing. (SCAPINO climbs out of boat and runs right,
followed by OTTAVIO.) Out with it, or you'll never blab
another secret again. (Chases OTTAVIO and SCAPINO
to stage right.)

SCAPINO.   Sir, you wouldn't mutilate me with a thing like
that, would you?

LEANDRO.   I would.

SCAPINO.   You wouldn't.

LEANDRO.   I'm waiting.

SCAPINO (putting OTTAVIO between him and
LEANDRO).   Yes, sir, but, I mean, what have I done?

LEANDRO.   You know. Your conscience tells you very well.

SCAPINO.   Honestly, sir, I swear I don't know. (LEANDRO
goes for SCAPINO. OTTAVIO falls to floor. LEANDRO
cartwheels over him.)

LEANDRO.   You know very well.

(First chase. SCAPINO runs down to lower corner of
forestage, then turns sharply toward table. LEANDRO
chases him all the way, while OTTAVIO tries to
intervene.)

OTTAVIO.   Leandro!

SCAPINO (leaping onto chair).   All right, all right. I confess
it was me who drank that small barrel of wine someone
gave you as a present a few days ago. I entertained a few
guests. It was me who made a hole in the barrel and poured
water all over the floor to make you think the wine had run
out.

LEANDRO.   So it was *you* who drank the wine and let me
scream at the servant girl thinking she was to blame.

SCAPINO.   Yes, sir. Yes, sir. I do hope that you will forgive
me.

LEANDRO.   I'm very glad to know about that, Scapino, but it doesn't happen to be what I'm after at the moment. (Swings at SCAPINO, who runs. LEANDRO misses him and, on backswing, hits OTTAVIO.)

(Second chase begins, this time through the water. The dialogue continues during the chase. SCAPINO runs upstage across the bridge, then across the center of the stage, past the cafe, and down the steps to the water, closely pursued by LEANDRO and OTTAVIO. When SCAPINO steps into the sea, OTTAVIO and LEANDRO stop in place and say "Ech!" then they follow suit. As they go through the sea, all hold their pants legs up and lift their knees high. SCAPINO races past the boat and climbs onto the forestage. He skirts the table and runs left, finally leaping off the stage by the barrels at left and running down the aisle into the audience. OTTAVIO and LEANDRO have followed but instead of going stage left, they run to the forestage steps.)

SCAPINO.   That's not it?
LEANDRO.   No. It's something more serious, and I'm determined to have it.
SCAPINO.   But I can't think of anything more serious, sir.
LEANDRO (going to hit him).   You won't say?
SCAPINO.   Oh . . .
OTTAVIO.   Gently there.
SCAPINO (in audience).   Look, I'm very sorry about this. All right, sir. I confess. Do you remember that little gold watch you gave to me to give to the gypsy girl you're in love with and I came back with my clothes torn to pieces and my face covered in blood and I told you some thugs had beaten me up and robbed me of that gold watch. (LEANDRO: "Well?") Well, it was me, sir. I wanted the gold watch myself.

LEANDRO.   But what could you possibly want my watch for?
SCAPINO.   To see what time it was.
LEANDRO.   I'm afraid you've not hit it yet.
SCAPINO.   That's still not it?
LEANDRO.   No, criminal. It's something more serious still.
SCAPINO.   Damnation!

(Third chase begins. SCAPINO runs out stage left into
    backstage area. OTTAVIO and LEANDRO run down the
    steps and follow. Then Leandro runs on stage from left,
    looking for SCAPINO. SCAPINO comes backing out of
    the cafe. LEANDRO, seeing him, runs after him.
    OTTAVIO comes out of cafe as SCAPINO leaps back in,
    and LEANDRO hits him by mistake.)

OTTAVIO.   Don't be so violent.

(They lock hands, spin three times in a circle; OTTAVIO falls
    into sea at stage center. SCAPINO runs around behind set
    to stage right. OTTAVIO clambers up on the forestage
    from the rear and spits water on himself. SCAPINO climbs
    ladder at stage right and enters balcony. OTTAVIO walks
    up to the laughing LEANDRO, who is still by the bench,
    and spits water in his face. LEANDRO runs after a
    laughing SCAPINO and climbs up to balcony. LEANDRO
    chases SCAPINO off balcony where SCAPINO hangs on
    rope.)

SCAPINO.   All right, sir, I confess it. Do you remember that
    ghost you met on the stairs a few weeks ago and nearly
    broke your neck falling backwards into the cellar running
    away?
LEANDRO.   Well? (With SCAPINO.) You were the ghost.
SCAPINO.   I was the ghost, sir . . . Just to frighten you a little
    bit to stop you from staying up all night keeping us running

around as you used to do. (LEANDRO hits SCAPINO
with sausage. SCAPINO falls off rope.)

LEANDRO. I'll remember all this at a proper time and place,
Scapino, but in the meantime come to the point and confess
exactly what you told my father.

SCAPINO. Told your father?

LEANDRO. Yes, my father.

SCAPINO. I haven't so much as seen him since his return.

LEANDRO. You've not?

SCAPINO. No, sir.

LEANDRO. Really?

SCAPINO. They'll tell you the same thing—I haven't seen
him.

LEANDRO. I have it from his own lips that . . .

SCAPINO. Well, excuse the expression, but his lips are not
telling the truth. (Sound of telephone bell ringing.)

(CARLO enters from cafe with old-fashioned, cordless
telephone and crosses right.)

CARLO. Pronto, pronto. (LEANDRO comes down from
balcony. SCAPINO goes and sits by the water, while
OTTAVIO comes down to CARLO.) Signore, signore,
terrible news. They're carrying her off.

LEANDRO (at bottom of ladder). Who? (Runs to CARLO.)

CARLO (listening on telephone). The gypsies are on the
point of running away with Zerbinetta. (LEANDRO and
OTTAVIO, on the sides of CARLO, take three steps
foward.) She's crying. (LEANDRO grabs receiver.
OTTAVIO holds base of telephone.)

LEANDRO. She never cries. (CARLO gets choked on wire
between base and receiver.)

CARLO (grabbing telephone back). She's crying now.
(Listens.) She says that if you don't get them the money the

gypsies have demanded for her within two hours, she will be gone from you forever. (Hangs up telephone.)

LEANDRO.   In two hours?

CARLO (listening again).   In two hours? ("Si.") Si, two hours. (Hangs up telephone. LEANDRO takes telephone and gives sausage to CARLO. Carlo gives sausage to OTTAVIO, takes telephone and goes back to cafe. OTTAVIO gives sausage to LEANDRO, who at first thinks it's the telephone and then throws it, hitting CARLO. A squeak as it hits.)

LEANDRO (moving toward SCAPINO).   Pronto, pronto, pronto, pronto . . . Dearest Scapino, give me your help. (SCAPINO escapes toward balcony. He fakes crying.)

SCAPINO.   "Dearest Scapino!" I'm dearest Scapino now that you need me.

LEANDRO (returning to bench).   I'll forgive you anything you've told me and anything worse you've done.

SCAPINO.   No, no, don't forgive me anything. Strangle me, stick a knife in me, beat me to death with a club. I'll enjoy every minute while you're killing me. (Kneels.)

LEANDRO.   No, I beg you to save my life in saving my love. (Kneels.)

SCAPINO.   Just finish me off quickly, that's all I ask. (On hands and knees.)

LEANDRO.   You're too deaf to me. I need your genius. (On hands and knees.)

SCAPINO.   Kill me. (Lies down.)

LEANDRO.   No. (Lies down.)

SCAPINO.   Just kill me. (Pushes up on hands and feet.)

LEANDRO.   No. (Pushes up on hands and feet.)

SCAPINO.   Just get it over with. (Flips onto back.)

LEANDRO.   No. (Flips onto back.)

OTTAVIO (lying on his back next to SCAPINO).   Scapino, you must do something to help.

SCAPINO (raising his head, then standing). What? After the way he insulted me?

LEANDRO (kneeling). Forget all that, I beg you, and give me your help.

OTTAVIO (kneeling). I join my petition to his.

SCAPINO (crossing downstage). I can still feel that insult deep down in here.

OTTAVIO. Put your pride on one side. (SCAPINO puts his pride on one side.)

LEANDRO (standing and crossing to SCAPINO, who moves away). Scapino, are you going to abandon me? In this cruel extremity? I was wrong. I admit that.

SCAPINO (crossing into forestage, approaching table). To treat me like a rogue, a villain, a scoundrel.

LEANDRO. I am more sorry than I can say . . .

SCAPINO (leaning on table). Yes, but . . . to hit me over the head . . . in public . . . with a . . . sausage.

LEANDRO. I beg your pardon with all my heart. And if that's not enough, I'll get down on my knees—(Kneeling.)— there, Scapino, and beg you once again to help me.

OTTAVIO (kneeling next to LEANDRO). You can't leave him now, Scapino. (They cry and beg SCAPINO, who milks it and makes them fall.)

SCAPINO. Well, yes. You get up. But next time don't be so quick with your accusations.

LEANDRO (he and OTTAVIO still kneeling). Will you get us out of this mess?

SCAPINO. I'll think about it.

LEANDRO. Well, you know time is pressing.

SCAPINO. Well, how much do you need?

LEANDRO. Five hundred thousand lire.

SCAPINO. And you?

OTTAVIO. Two hundred thousand.

SCAPINO (going upstage). Good, I shall get these out of your dads. (LEANDRO and OTTAVIO stand. To

OTTAVIO.) As to yours, the plan's already made. (To
LEANDRO.) And as for yours, first-class miser though he
is, there'll be even less trouble. He's not exactly an Einstein.
He's the sort of fella you can con into almost anything.

LEANDRO.   How dare you!

SCAPINO.   Now don't get upset. You know there's not the
slightest resemblance between you and him. And you know
perfectly well that everybody knows he's only your father
because he happened to be married to your mother at the
time.

LEANDRO.   Scapino!

ARGANTE (offstage left).   Of all the ridiculous behavior.

LEANDRO.   Shush, Scapino!

SCAPINO.   But here comes your father, Ottavio. We'll start
the deal with him since he's here first. You get along and
tell Sylvestro to come at a trot ready to play his part. (Exit
OTTAVIO and LEANDRO into cafe. They peek out until
ARGANTE passes, then duck out of sight.)

(ARGANTE enters left and makes a long cross to right.)

ARGANTE (to himself, crossing to stage right).   No good
sense . . . no consideration. To jump headlong into
marriage like this. Oh, the follies of youth.

SCAPINO (under stage right balcony).   Your servant, signor.

ARGANTE.   How do, Scapino.

SCAPINO.   You're having a little think about your son's
situation, are you?

ARGANTE (crossing downstage).   I must admit it's put me in
a state of fury.

SCAPINO (following him).   Life, sir, is full of disappointments.
It's best to be prepared for them.

ARGANTE (at forestage left).   That's all very well, but this
foolish marriage has spoiled all our plans, and I'm not

going to stand for it. And I've already been to see about
getting it dissolved. (*Goes down the stairs.*)

SCAPINO (*at center of forestage*).   No, sir, if you'll only listen
to me, you'll find another way of settling this. You know
what going to law means in this country? You'll find
yourself stuck into so many complications and costs . . .
(*ARGANTE comes up onto forestage again.*)

ARGANTE.   Costs! That's true. That's very true. But what
other way is there?

SCAPINO (*offering ARGANTE a seat, which he takes*).   I
think I've one. I've just been chatting to the brother of the
girl Ottavio's married. He's one of these roughnecks, one of
these toughs who stand around the street corners poking
people on the nose, beating them with chains, talking about
nothing but punching and slashing and shooting, standing
there with cut-throat razors waiting for streakers, and
thinks no more of killing a bloke than drinking a glass of
wine. I got him round to talking about the marriage. I
dropped a hint to him how easy it would be to dissolve it on
account of the gun at the ceremony, and how your influence
in the city, your bank balance and your powerful friends
would help you along in court. Anyway, I got him to listen
to a little proposal I made for settling the whole thing for a
small consideration, and he agrees that the marriage should
be dissolved providing he gets the money. (*Goes back up to
bridge.*)

ARGANTE (*standing*).   And how much did he ask?

SCAPINO.   Ooh, at first, a fantastic sum.

ARGANTE.   Well, tell me.

SCAPINO.   Oh, you wouldn't believe it.

ARGANTE (*going to foot of bridge*).   But tell me what.

SCAPINO.   He said . . . he said . . . he wouldn't settle for less
than five or six hundred thousand lire.

ARGANTE.   Five or six hundred . . . (*On bridge, beside*

SCAPINO.) The devil seize him. Does he think I'm an
idiot?

SCAPINO (imitating ARGANTE behind his back). That's
just what I said to him. I said to him, "Do you think that
man is an idiot?" I said you weren't as much an idiot as you
looked and after a lot more arguing he agrees to settle for
. . . enough to pay off his landlady so he can collect his
luggage—a mere two hundred thousand lire.

ARGANTE. Two hundred thousand lire?

SCAPINO. Yes.

ARGANTE (walking about forestage in a rage). Come on,
we'll go to court. (He goes down forestage steps and up the
steps left toward cafe.)

SCAPINO. Oh, oh, think, sir.

ARGANTE (going up stairs by the boat). I'll go to court.
(SCAPINO approaches ARGANTE by crossing bridge
and going left.)

SCAPINO. Now don't go jumping head-first into . . .

ARGANTE (continuing off left). I'll go to court.

SCAPINO. You know that going to court will cost you money.

(ARGANTE runs back on stage.)

ARGANTE. Money? (He stops by the steps of the boat
landing.)

SCAPINO (taking ARGANTE by the shoulder and running
him back on forestage). Not to mention the little bits here
and there for greasing of palms. Give the man the money
and you've settled the whole thing.

ARGANTE. But two hundred thousand lire.

SCAPINO. Yes, and you'll make a profit.

ARGANTE (turning to SCAPINO). Profit! (SCAPINO
offers ARGANTE a chair again, which he takes.
SCAPINO sits opposite him.)

SCAPINO.   Yes, a profit. I've just been doing a quick
calculation in my head of all the legal costs and I've worked
out that in giving your man two hundred thousand lire
you'll save at least a hundred and fifty thousand over and
above that without reckoning all the worries and anxieties,
time wasting and vexation you'll cause yourself. Even if it
saved you all the cheeky things the lawyers will write about
you that could well appear in the *Women's Wear Daily*, it
could be worth three hundred thousand not to go to law.

ARGANTE.   I don't care a damn, I defy any lawyer to make
an idiot of me.

SCAPINO (standing).   . . . Then do what you will, sir. (Walks
away.)

(SCAPINO whistles for SYLVESTRO, who enters cafe balcony
left in leathers with a bicycle chain.)

SCAPINO.   . . . but if I were you I'd avoid the law.

ARGANTE.   I'm not giving away two hundred thousand lire.

SCAPINO.   Ah! (Getting ARGANTE to look at cafe
balcony.)

SYLVESTRO (on balcony).   Hey, hey, Scapino, come and
show me where this rat Argante, Ottavio's father, is. (Exits
balcony.)

SCAPINO (returning to table).   Why, old chap . . . Sir, do
you know who that is? That's the brother of the girl Ottavio
married; who stands on street corners going . . .

(Enter SYLVESTRO from cafe, imitating a bouncing thug.)

SYLVESTRO (crossing to center).   You deaf or something?
Come and show me where that rat Argante, Ottavio's
father, is.

SCAPINO (as he and ARGANTE stand).   Why, old chap?

SYLVESTRO.   I've just heard he's gonna take me to court,
   and dissolve by law the marriage of my sister.

SCAPINO.   I don't know whether he intends to do that, but I
   do know he won't pay you two hundred thousand lire. He
   says it's far too much. (SYLVESTRO moves in and back
   again, swinging his fists and chain. ARGANTE tries to run
   off left. SCAPINO stops him.)

SYLVESTRO (continuing to pace and swing chain).   I'll kill
   him . . . Off with his head . . . Off with his appendages. If
   I find him, I'll make mincemeat of him, even if I get the
   chair for it. (Banging into right chair.)

SCAPINO.   But, sir, Ottavio's father has guts and maybe he
   won't be frightened of you.

SYLVESTRO (coming to lower end of bridge).   Him? Him?
   Blood and giblets. If he was standing there now, I'd wrap
   my chain 'round his chops in no time at all. (Sees
   ARGANTE.) Who's that man there?

SCAPINO (pushing ARGANTE forward toward
   SYLVESTRO).   Oh, this man, that's not him; that's not
   him.

SYLVESTRO.   Are you sure it isn't a friend of Argante?

SCAPINO.   A friend? No, no. This man is his deadliest enemy.

SYLVESTRO.   His deadliest enemy? (As ARGANTE makes
   like a deadly enemy, clawing.)

SCAPINO.   Yes.

SYLVESTRO.   Well, you old sonofabitch, glad to'meet you. So
   you're a deadly enemy of that fellow Argante, eh?

SCAPINO (going to table and leaning on it).   Yes, I'll answer
   for him.

SYLVESTRO.   Shake, buster, shake. (ARGANTE shakes all
   over.) I give you my word, I'll swear on my honor, by the
   chain I carry, by the razor in my pocket, by all the
   saints—(Spitting in his own hand, and crossing to
   ARGANTE.)—that before this day's finished I'll rid you of
   that sniveling scoundrel, that stool pigeon Argante. You

can depend on me. (They shake hands. Both react and
wipe off spit.)

SCAPINO.   But, sir, violence is against the law in this country.

SYLVESTRO.   What do I care? What have I got to lose?

SCAPINO.   But he has friends and relatives who'll protect him
against you.

SYLVESTRO.   That's just what I want. Gaawd. (Moving back
upstage. He swings chain and does a mock attack as though
there are lots of people around him.) Off with his head;
right across the belly. If only he was here right now with all
his friends and relations! Just let him get near with thirty
policemen! Let 'em all come, truncheons, pistols, and all!
(He stands on his guard.) Okay, you guys, fight to the
finish. Come on, rats, fight to kill. No prisoners. Slash!
(Leaps toward table, miming fight.) Bang! Strangle!
Worms! Chickens! If that's what you want, I'll give you
your bellyful. One down, pow, pow, pop, two down, pow,
pow. (Threatens ARGANTE and SCAPINO.) Frightened,
eh? (Hitting chain on table.)

SCAPINO.   Sir, we're on your side, sir.

SYLVESTRO (moving back upstage).   Well, that just shows
you what happens to anybody who gets on the wrong side
of me. (Bangs into bench, puts his hands up.) I beg your
pardon. (Turns, sees it's the bench, hits it with chain, exits
cafe.)

SCAPINO (moving right).   That just shows you how many
men can be killed for a mere two hundred thousand lire. Oi
vey, I'm off! (Exits stage right stairs.)

ARGANTE (crossing to bridge, trembling).
Sca . . . Sca . . . Sca . . . Sca . . . Sca . . .
Sca . . . Sca . . . Scapino!

(SCAPINO reenters up stairs.)

SCAPINO (moving to ARGANTE).   Pino . . . pino . . .
pino, sir . . . pino.

ARGANTE.   I've changed my mind. I think I'll give him the
    money.
SCAPINO.   Sir, I'm delighted, for your sake.
ARGANTE (taking out wallet).   Let's go and find him; I've
    got the money with me.
SCAPINO.   No, sir, all you have to do is give the money to me.
    It's not possible for you to meet him, not after pretending to
    be somebody else; and I'm afraid knowing you've tricked
    him, he might decide to ask for more.
ARGANTE.   True, true, but I'd feel a lot happier to see what
    happened to my money.
SCAPINO.   Don't you trust me, sir?
ARGANTE.   Oh, no, no, it's not that, but . . .
SCAPINO (returning to stairs).   Now, sir, either I'm a rogue
    or I'm an honest man; one or the other. Why should I want
    to trick you? It's only to help you and my master that I'm
    risking all this. (ARGANTE moves down to him.) If you
    don't trust me, then I'll wash my hands of the whole thing
    and you'd better find someone else to do your dirty work for
    you.
ARGANTE (trying to give him the money).   No, you take the
    money.
SCAPINO (refusing it).   No, sir, I'll be very happy if you give
    it to someone else.
ARGANTE.   Take it! I beg you.
SCAPINO.   No. How do you know I won't trick you out of
    your money?
ARGANTE.   For God's sake, take it. Don't make me argue
    any more . . . I'll go and wait for you at home. (Hands
    money to SCAPINO, goes upstage and across toward cafe.)
SCAPINO.   I'll be there shortly. (ARGANTE exits upstage.)

(SYLVESTRO enters cafe balcony.)

SYLVESTRO.   Ciao!
SCAPINO.   Ciao! (Repeat Ciao!) One down, one to go. (Sits
    at table counting money.)
SYLVESTRO.   Hey, here he comes now.

(SYLVESTRO exits into cafe as GERONTE approaches from
    stage right aisle.)

SCAPINO (jumping up, putting money away).   Oh, God,
    heaven's got them queueing up today. (Running about,
    pretending he hasn't seen GERONTE.) Poor old fellow!
    Poor old Geronte. Poor old chap. What'll he do?
GERONTE (onto forestage via steps).   What's he saying about
    me? With a face like a lemon.
SCAPINO (running upstage and to bench).   Can anyone tell
    me where to find poor, poor Signor Geronte?
GERONTE (going upstage as SCAPINO runs down).   What's
    the matter, Scapino? (They have passed each other,
    SCAPINO now being at lower edge of forestage.)
SCAPINO (running left).   If only I could find him to tell him
    about this terrible disaster.
GERONTE.   What on earth is it?
SCAPINO.   I've searched everywhere for him, but all in vain.
GERONTE (down to bridge).   I'm here! . . . It's me.
SCAPINO (running to edge of forestage and peering over).
    Maybe he is hiding under the quay and nobody can find
    him.
GERONTE (coming up behind him and poking him with
    umbrella).   Hey, are you deaf?
SCAPINO.   Sir! It's impossible to find you anywhere, sir.
GERONTE.   I've been standing right behind you for the past
    hour. What on earth is it, whatever it is?
SCAPINO.   Sir.
GERONTE.   What?

SCAPINO. Sir, your son . . .

GERONTE. Go on. My son . . .

SCAPINO. Your son has got himself mixed up in the most
extraordinary business in the whole world.

GERONTE. Whatever's that?

SCAPINO (joining GERONTE on bridge). Well, I saw him a
short while ago looking upset, very unhappy, at something
you must have said to him, in which for no good reason you
managed to get me involved; and seeking to take his mind
off his troubles, I took him for a walk along the quayside.
(He walks GERONTE upstage.) There we were, admiring
the boats, one of them in particular, a beautiful
motor-yacht, when up came a young fellow, Turkish he
was, what a delight, shook us by the hand and invited us on
board. (They sit on bench.) So on we went. We ate the
most beautiful food, and drank wine such as you've never
tasted.

GERONTE. Well, how did this make you feel so bad?

SCAPINO. Just a minute, just a minute, sir! While we were
eating and drinking, he ordered the boat to put to sea and
when we were a good way from the harbor he threw me
overboard into the skiff—(Jumps into boat.)—and sent me
to tell you that if you don't send him by return by me five
hundred thousand lire he'll kidnap your son and sail him off
to Algiers.

GERONTE (jumping up). What the devil . . . five hundred
thousand lire!

SCAPINO. Yes, sir, and not only that, he's given me only two
hours to get it. No, I'm a liar, one hour and fifty minutes.

GERONTE. Oh, that terror of a Turk, he'll be the death of
me.

SCAPINO (climbing out of boat). You must tell me, sir, how
to rescue your son who you love so tenderly from a fate
worse than death.

GERONTE (stamping foot). What the devil was he doing on board that boat?

SCAPINO. Well, he didn't realize this was going to happen, did he, sir?

GERONTE. Off with you, Scapino, off with you, and tell that Turk I'll send the police after him.

SCAPINO (running off, then stopping on the bridge). The police, sir, what a good idea. . . . The police? In the middle of the ocean? Look, you must be having a joke with me.

GERONTE (stamping foot). What the devil was he doing on board that boat?

SCAPINO. Well . . . ah . . . some people have bad luck, sir.

GERONTE. Scapino, the time has come when you must play the part of a faithful servant.

SCAPINO (returning to GERONTE). Yes, sir.

GERONTE. Go along, and ask this Turk to send me back my son, and tell him I've sent you to take my son's place until I've got enough cash together.

SCAPINO (running off again and then again stopping on bridge). What an idea . . . what an idea, sir! . . . Do you really know what you're talking about?

GERONTE. No . . .

SCAPINO. Do you expect that Turk to have so little savvy as to swap your son for a wretch like me?

GERONTE (stamping foot). What the devil was he doing on board that boat?

SCAPINO (imitating GERONTE). Well, he didn't know it was going to happen, did he? Just think, sir, he only gave me an hour and a half.

GERONTE. You say he asks . . .

SCAPINO (crossing to GERONTE with hand out for money). Five hundred thousand lire.

GERONTE. Five hundred thousand lire.

SCAPINO.   Yes.

GERONTE.   Has he no conscience?

SCAPINO.   Certainly. The conscience of a Turk. (Both laugh, then to audience:)

SCAPINO and GERONTE.   That's not funny!

GERONTE.   Does he think that money like that is just picked up in the gutter?

SCAPINO.   Some people have no business sense.

GERONTE.   But what the devil was he doing on board that boat?

SCAPINO (moving downstage).   Yes . . . Yes . . . Quite right. But one doesn't read fortunes, does one, sir? Look . . . Come on, let's get it over with.

GERONTE (taking key out of pocket and going to SCAPINO).   All right. Here's the key of my closet.

SCAPINO (meeting GERONTE).   Good. (Takes the key.)

GERONTE.   Open it.

SCAPINO.   What? The key?

GERONTE.   The closet.

SCAPINO.   Oh, very good.

GERONTE.   Inside you'll find a little hook. On the hook you'll find a big key which unlocks the attic. Inside you'll find a larger key which is the key to my secret hidey hole. Go in there and you'll see a large brass bedstead. On the bed there is a mattress. Lift it up, roll it over, sell it and use the money to ransom my son.

SCAPINO.   Sell it. You wouldn't get a hundred lire for a mattress, and please think how little time there is.

GERONTE.   *What* the *devil* was he *doing* on board that *boat?*

SCAPINO.   Quite right; but forget the boat. Drop the boat. Because by this time you've almost lost your son. (Gives key back to GERONTE and goes left. He bursts into tears.) Poor, poor, poor fellow. I may never see you again. They're sailing you off to Algiers to a fate we wot not of. But heaven's my witness—(Falls on knees.)—I've done all

I could, and there's none to blame but a hard-hearted
father.

GERONTE (crossing right). Don't strain yourself, Scapino.
I'll go and get the money.

SCAPINO (now by the boat). Then hurry, sir. I tremble lest
the clock strikes.

GERONTE (stopping under the balcony and turning). Was it
four hundred thousand you said?

SCAPINO. No, no, five hundred thousand.

GERONTE. Five hundred thousand?

SCAPINO. Yes.

GERONTE. *What* the *devil* was he *doing* on *board* that *boat?*

SCAPINO. Quite right, but hurry up.

GERONTE. *Blast* that *boat.*

SCAPINO (to audience). That boat's going to give him a
heart attack.

GERONTE (crossing to SCAPINO). Here, Scapino. I've
remembered someone's paid me money . . . I never
dreamed it'd be leaving me so soon. Here, take it. Ransom
my son. (Puts money on SCAPINO's outstretched hand.)

SCAPINO. Sir.

GERONTE. But tell that Turk he's a devil. (More money.)

SCAPINO. Yes, sir!

GERONTE. A murderer. (More money.)

SCAPINO. Certainly, sir.

GERONTE. A money-grabber. (More money.)

SCAPINO. Just you leave it to me, sir.

GERONTE (more money). And if I ever catch him I'll have
my revenge on him. (Takes all money and goes right.)

SCAPINO (calling after him). Just a minute, sir. . . .
Where's the money?

GERONTE. I gave it to you.

SCAPINO. No, no. . . . You put it back in your wallet.

GERONTE. I put it back in my wallet?

SCAPINO. You put it back in your wallet.

GERONTE.   In my wallet . . . I put it back in my wallet. . . .
(Crossing to SCAPINO and giving him the money, wallet
and all.) Ah, it's grief disturbs my senses.

SCAPINO.   That's plain to see.

GERONTE (crossing right).   *What* the *devil* was he *doing* on
board that *boat? Blast* the *boat.* That *terror* of a *Turk*, he'll
be the *death* of *me.* (Stops a moment, facing audience.
SCAPINO stands on bench, encouraging audience to join
in.)

SCAPINO and GERONTE.   *What* the *devil* was he *doing*
board that *boat?*

GERONTE.   I hate Turks. (Exits right.)

SCAPINO.   I'm not through with you yet, you old miser. I'll
pay you back in another form of coin for the tale you told
about me to your son. (Crosses downstage to bridge.)

(Enter OTTAVIO and LEANDRO from left in bathing suits,
flippers, masks, snorkels. They jump in sea and swim to
SCAPINO.)

OTTAVIO (up on bridge, removing mask and flippers).   Well,
Scapino, any success? (LEANDRO jumps out of water
farther upstage and takes off mask and flippers.)

SCAPINO (to OTTAVIO).   Two hundred thousand lire.

OTTAVIO (standing and taking money).   I'm wild with
happiness.

LEANDRO.   And have you done anything to save my love
from disaster?

SCAPINO (to LEANDRO).   Sir, for you, I could do nothing
. . .

LEANDRO (running into cafe and up to balcony).   Then I
must end it all. Life means nothing to me without my lovely
Zerbinetta. (At balcony, climbing over rail, threatening to
jump.) What else can I do? I must end it all. (OTTAVIO
and SCAPINO run to left, look up at balcony.)

SCAPINO.   What's he talking about? . . . No, no. Wait. Take
     it easy. I was only joking. . . . Sir, stop it. Here, will this
     settle your difficulties? (Holding out money.)
LEANDRO.   You've made life worth living.
SCAPINO (to OTTAVIO).   Get him down. (OTTAVIO
     helps LEANDRO down. SCAPINO holds out money, then
     pulls it back.) On one condition. That you allow me a little
     revenge on your father for this trick he's played on me.
LEANDRO (reaching for money).   Anything you like.
SCAPINO (pulling money back).   You swear it, in front of
     witnii?
LEANDRO.   Yes.
SCAPINO (giving LEANDRO money).   Five hundred
     thousand lire. (Exits cafe.)
LEANDRO.   Come on, let's go and buy the lovely creature
     that I *love*.
OTTAVIO.   My lovely Giacinta. (Puts mask back on.)
LEANDRO.   My lovely Zerbinetta. (Puts mask back on. They
     jump into sea, lie down as if in water. Then both stand, lift
     masks, and shout their own sound effects.)
OTTAVIO and LEANDRO.   Splash! (They bow and swim off
     stage left.)

                         END OF PART ONE

the intermission

HEADWAITER and WAITER 1 enter from cafe, move bench into Part Two position and cross to the table and chairs on forestage. WAITRESS enters yawning, puts five coins in jukebox and starts music as she did previously. She moves chair from left table to right of jukebox and returns to cafe. WAITERS start the following routine: wearily they put the chairs on top of the table and carry table, chairs and all upstage. As they run into obstacles (steps, ramps, etc.) they can't pass, they put table down, remove chairs, carry table and chairs separately over obstacle, and then put chairs back on table carrying the whole load to the next obstacle where they repeat the process. WAITRESS enters eating a large hero-type sandwich and sits in chair by jukebox watching them. Moving down the last obstacle, the WAITERS, not judging the weight of the table correctly, lose control and crash through the cafe doors. They come back out, put table and chairs upstage of cafe. HEADWAITER, going back into cafe, notices WAITRESS and "giving her a look" tells her to get up and motions WAITER 1 to put chair with the others. HEADWAITER exits. WAITER 1, "coming on" to WAITRESS throughout, takes chair with one hand—showing his strength—and puts it away. He goes back to WAITRESS and she begins stroking and massaging his right arm, which he raises in the air flexing its muscle. The WAITRESS crosses by him leading him toward cafe. He follows with arm held in flexed position. At cafe entrance, she turns to him, nods her head and both exit quickly into cafe.

part two

(The jukebox is still playing. Seagulls are heard. The stage is
clear. The NURSE enters the auditorium from the front of
the house with the last of the audience, and moves down the
right aisle toward the stage; crosses in front of the forestage
to the left stairs by the boat; walks up the stairs and looks in
the garbage barrel. HEADWAITER and WAITER 1 come
into the cafe balcony and begin playing a game, one hiding
chalk in his closed hands, the other trying to guess which
hand it's in. The NURSE tiptoes through the sea toward the
forestage. WAITERS stop game and watch NURSE.
NURSE wipes muck off shoes and crosses to center of
forestage, where she leans over and looks into sea, then
looks behind her at audience and fixes her dress. She then
crosses to bridge. WAITRESS enters from cafe, eating the
last of her sandwich, and leans against post of cafe balcony
watching NURSE. Now near the bridge, the NURSE hears
a whistle. It comes from the cafe balcony. NURSE thinks
it's from the audience; stops, turns, makes a quiet "puss" at
someone. Receives no reactions and crosses left toward
cafe. In front of cafe she sees WAITRESS, stops, crosses
herself, turns around, crosses to bench, takes out a hanky,
cleans bench and sits. WAITERS return to game. CARLO
enters balcony, begins participating in game. WAITER 1
sides with CARLO, loses and smacks CARLO on the
shoulder. The sound of guitar strumming is heard as

SCAPINO enters balcony with guitar. The seagulls fade.
SCAPINO is about to start singing "O Sole Mio"; CARLO
breaks out into song first:

O SOLE MIO

O Sole Mio (CARLO sings by himself)
Chow Chow Bambino
Three Pounds Per Kilo
Serra Serra

Pastrami, Frank Dunlopillo (SCAPINO and WAITER
      1 join CARLO)
Ajax et Brillo
An' Tony Quinn

La Dolche Vita
Sophia Ponte
Moonlight in Vermonte
Serra Serra
Chinzano et Mia Farrow
Until tomarrow
Chow Chow for Now
      Ole! (A shout)

LEANDRO and OTTAVIO enter from cafe dancing
together and drinking chianti. They stop dancing left of
bench. LEANDRO drinks. OTTAVIO takes bottle, drinks
and leads LEANDRO off, dangling the bottle. Song ends.
SCAPINO continues strumming guitar as he and
WAITERS hum slow version of "Minestrone Macaroni."
As song ends, CARLO leaves balcony, runs down stairs
and enters from cafe, ice cream box hanging from neck,
scoop in hand. "Gelati, Gelati!" WAITRESS enters cafe.
CARLO crosses right. "Gelati molta, molta freddo." He

stops right of NURSE. She signals for an ice cream, stands, crosses to him. He opens ice cream box; she points inside; he whispers in her ear. She reacts violently, hits him on head with handbag and exits to cafe. CARLO crosses left and down steps by boat; "Gelati, Gelati, chocolata, vanilla, molta flavores, cento flavores, Baskein Robins." GIACINTA, ZERBINETTA and SYLVESTRO enter right humming the same as men of balcony and miming mandolin play with forefinger in front of mouth. GIACINTA turns to cross down bridge to forestage; SYLVESTRO sits on bench; ZERBINETTA is at right of bench. CARLO crosses to forestage: "Chocolata a fudge ripple"; seeing GIACINTA: "Gelati, signorina." They cross and meet. CARLO opens gelati box. GIACINTA looks in, points to a flavor, and CARLO fixes her a cone. He starts to give it to her, looks at her breasts, reaches into box with scoop and puts another scoop on cone and gives it to her. He backs away from her and ZERBINETTA crosses down to bridge. CARLO, moving away from GIACINTA, takes out cone for next customer with his right hand. As he turns, the cone is crushed on ZERBINETTA's left breast. He takes out another cone, saying "Hagen Daze," fixes some ice cream on it, and gives cone to her singing "Hagen Daze are here again" and backs upstage still looking at ZERBINETTA who sits above bridge. As he reaches the bench he takes out a dixie cup and bangs it against SYLVESTRO's face. SYLVESTRO takes the cup. CARLO puts out his hand for money. SYLVESTRO takes lid off cup and puts it sticky-side down on CARLO's out-stretched hand. CARLO, still looking at ZERBINETTA, puts lid in his chest pocket, bangs gelati box into SYLVESTRO, and finally, still looking at ZERBINETTA, walks [gelati box first] into cafe wall, gelati box hitting him in groin. He doubles over and exits into cafe. SCAPINO and WAITERS stop humming and

exit balcony. [Following scene should have a quiet
romantic atmosphere.])

SYLVESTRO.   Yes, and your two young men have agreed that
you should stay together, and I am carrying out the order
they have given me.

GIACINTA (eating ice cream; to ZERBINETTA).   Such an
order does nothing but please me. I am happy to have you
as my companion, and it shall not be my fault if the
friendship between those we love is not echoed between us
two.

(SCAPINO enters from cafe, takes ice cream from
SYLVESTRO, crosses and sits in chair at right table.)

ZERBINETTA (eating ice cream).   I agree, and I am not
someone to refuse an offer of friendship.

SCAPINO.   And when that offer is love?

ZERBINETTA.   Love is another matter. There is a little more
risk and I'm not so brave.

SCAPINO.   Yes, well, I wish you'd take that risk for my master
now. What he has just done for you should make you brave
enough.

ZERBINETTA.   What he has just done is not quite enough to
convince me. We're just good friends. (Laughs.) I may be
always smiling and full of laughter, but for all my laughing,
I am serious on certain matters and your master mistakes
himself if he thinks his having bought me means he owns
me. He will have to fortify his love with certain ceremonies
thought necessary on these occasions. (GIACINTA crosses
and sits in prow of boat.)

SCAPINO.   That's just what he intends to do. His intentions
are strictly honorable. If a sinful thought had entered his
head, do you think I would be mixed up in the business?

ZERBINETTA.   I long to believe you, but I can see certain
objections coming from his father.
SCAPINO.   Well, we'll soon sort those out.
GIACINTA (to ZERBINETTA).   The similarity of our
adventures should make us still more friends; we both suffer
the same apprehensions, and are exposed to the same
misfortunes. Well, cheer up, we're both in the same boat.
ZERBINETTA.   But at least you have the advantage of
knowing who were your parents, and that one day you can
find them again; they can consent to your marriage and set
everything to rights. But what I am makes it impossible for
me to gain the favor of his father, who respects only money.
GIACINTA.   But at least you have the advantage that your
lover is not tempted to make another marriage.
ZERBINETTA.   A change of mind is the least to fear in a
lover. It's natural to believe one's attractions will keep their
interest. The real enemy is an interfering father, for whom
one's attractions have no interest at all. Heigho.
GIACINTA.   Heigh . . . ho!
SYLVESTRO.   Heigh . . . ho!
GIACINTA.   What crosses we true lovers must bear.
(GIACINTA, ZERBINETTA and SYLVESTRO sigh with
mouths open.) How delicious to be in love—(Sighs.)—
with nothing to disturb the beating of two hearts together.
(Sighs. SCAPINO laughs crudely and stands.)
SCAPINO (crossing to center of forestage).   Don't delude
yourself. A peaceful love affair is a boring one. You need
your ups and downs. Troubles in love make us appreciate
the pleasures and make us love even more. (GIACINTA
and ZERBINETTA sigh.)
ZERBINETTA (crossing down to SCAPINO).   Enough,
Scapino; help us forget our troubles by making us laugh.
GIACINTA.   Mmm. (She also comes to forestage.)
SYLVESTRO.   Yes.

SCAPINO.   No, no, no.

ZERBINETTA.   Tell us the story of how you got the money
out of the old miser.

SCAPINO.   No, they heard it.

ZERBINETTA.   Oh, come on. (Girls tickle his legs.)

SCAPINO.   Stop it. Look, it's all right at rehearsal; but not on
the night . . . Now, I told you, didn't I . . . Sylvestro can
. . . (ZERBINETTA tickles him again.) . . . Cut your
nails . . . Look, Sylvestro can tell you that story as well as
I. At the moment I'm trying to think up a little revenge on
old Geronte. (The girls walk up and cross stage to area
above boat.)

SYLVESTRO (moving quickly to SCAPINO).   Why, just
when we're all happy, do you want to get yourself mixed up
in another load of trouble?

SCAPINO.   Because it makes me happier still to risk my
chance.

SYLVESTRO.   I've told you before, you'll give up that plan if
you'll take any notice of me.

SCAPINO.   Who takes any notice of you?

SYLVESTRO.   Now why the devil do you need to amuse
yourself in that way?

SCAPINO.   And why the devil do you need to worry about it?

SYLVESTRO.   'Cause I don't like to see you, unless it's a real
case of necessity, getting yourself a good hiding.

SCAPINO.   Look, it will be my good hiding, not yours.

SYLVESTRO (crossing upstage and to girls).   All right, all
right. Your hiding's your own affair.

SCAPINO.   Look, I've never been stopped by danger. I just
can't stand those boasters who are so busy working out the
risks they are going to take, they don't take any.

ZERBINETTA.   Hey, Scapino, we'll be needing your help.

SCAPINO.   Yes, well, I'll be along in a couple of shakes of a
. . .

ZERBINETTA.   A what?

SCAPINO.   How's your father? [An English expression
   meaning, "Whatever you want it to be."]
SYLVESTRO (exiting upstage with GIACINTA and
   ZERBINETTA).   Ciao!
SCAPINO.   Ciao!
OTHERS.   Ciao!
SCAPINO.   Ciao!
OTHERS.   Ciao!
SCAPINO.   Oh, Ciao! (Exit SYLVESTRO, GIACINTA and
   ZERBINETTA.) Nobody's going to say that I give away
   secrets . . .

(Enter WAITER 1 from cafe, carrying a large sack.)

SCAPINO.   . . . and get away with it. (WAITER, with sack,
   is picking up paper and putting it in. At bench he begins
   singing a sentimental Irish song. He continues on
   downstage, where SCAPINO picks up paper, throws it in
   sack and joining in on second round of song, takes the
   sack. Song ends. SCAPINO begins clapping, audience
   claps. WAITER takes embarrassed bow, crosses upstage,
   bows again, exits cafe. SCAPINO is now downstage with
   the sack. He opens it, looks in and pulls out sausage. He
   puts down sausage and sack, devising plan.)

(GERONTE enters right and crosses downstage toward
   SCAPINO.)

GERONTE.   Well, Scapino, how are you getting on with
   saving my son?
SCAPINO.   Your son, your son, is now perfectly safe. But it's
   you who now run the risk. You're in the greatest danger,
   sir. What I wouldn't do to see you locked up safely back
   home.
GERONTE.   Why?

SCAPINO.   Why, at this very moment, sir, they're searching
    everywhere to murder you.
GERONTE.   Me?
SCAPINO.   Yes.
GERONTE.   Who?
SCAPINO.   The brother of the girl Ottavio married. He thinks
    that your plan to put your daughter in the marriage bed
    reserved for his sister will succeed. Thinking this, he's
    determined to wreak vengeance on you and make you pay
    with your life for the slight on his family's honor. At this
    moment all his friends, bullies like himself, they are
    questioning every person in this town. I myself saw a squad
    of soldiers, all friends of his, beating up and questioning
    people, and laying siege to every way back to your house so
    that you can't get home or take a step to right or left
    without falling into their hands.
GERONTE.   My dear Scapino, what shall I do?
SCAPINO.   Well, I don't know, sir, do I? It's a funny situation.
    I'm so frightened for you I'm trembling from hand to
    mouth. (He pretends to go and look up every alley, then
    claps his hands.) Sir, I have it. I have a way to rescue you.
    But first you must get into that sack.
GERONTE.   Oh, noooo.
SCAPINO.   Ah! Oh, my God, look over there!
GERONTE (jumping into sack, in fear).   Who is it?
SCAPINO.   Good, good, now you there, all you have to do is
    get to the bottom of that sack. Don't make a sound. Don't
    make a move. I can then lift you up, you see, as if you were
    a bundle. Put you on my back, carry you through your
    enemies back to your house where we can then barricade
    ourselves in and then phone for the police.
GERONTE (getting down in sack).   A brilliant idea.
SCAPINO (helping him).   None better, sir. That's it. In you
    go, sir, all the way to the bottom, sir, and do not make a
    sound whatever happens.

GERONTE.   Just leave it to me. I'll not even breathe.

SCAPINO.   Good, good, all the way to the bottom, sir. That's it. (GERONTE is now in sack. However, his umbrella is sticking out. SCAPINO pushes it in, sticking GERONTE who yells.) . . . Just in time, sir, just in time. Here's a real villainous-looking one. . . . Now do not make a sound whatever happens. . . . He's a . . . he's just sailing up in a boat. (Takes sausage, runs into boat and picks up broom, fixes hat as a pirate, jumps out of boat using broom as a crutch, starts walking to the sack with parrot [imaginary] on shoulder, and takes on assumed voice.)

SCAPINO (as LONG JOHN SILVER).   Ah ha! Sixteen men on a dead man's chest. Yo ho ho and a bottle of gin. Avast there, ye landlubbers—can any man Jack of you tell me, Long John Silver, where I can find that pirate, Geronte. ("Pretty Polly.") Shut up, you. You over there, you with the sack, it's Jim lad, isn't it? You tell me where I can find this Geronte, Jim, and I'll give ye a gold balloon—I'll give ye a gold doubloon.

SCAPINO (as himself).   Sir, sir, are you searching for my very good friend, Signor Geronte?

SCAPINO (as LONG JOHN SILVER).   Ay, that I am, lad, so that I can keel, haul him, hang him from the highest yardarm, peck him to death with my parrot. ("Pretty Polly.") Shut up, you, or I'll stuff you.

SCAPINO.   Sir, I do not know where Signor Geronte is.

SCAPINO (as LONG JOHN SILVER).   Jim, lad, you don't happen to be a shipmate of his, do ye?

SCAPINO.   Yes, sir, yes, sir. "I do ye." A very devoted shipmate.

SCAPINO (as LONG JOHN SILVER).   Right then, Jim— then you take this to him from me—("Pretty Polly.")—and her, too. (Attacks the sack, shouting, etc., as if he were being beaten.) Ar, you let that be a lesson to you, Jim. Tell this Geronte that when I find him he'll be my

little bit of treasure, and you know what a pirate does with
a little bit of treasure? ("He buries it.") He buries it. Right.
So now I'm off. Up sail, up anchor. Up, up and away in my
beautiful doubloon . . . up into the sky . . . (SCAPINO
lies down and begins screaming.)

SCAPINO.   Sir, ooh, damn the bully, may they take his guts
for garters.

GERONTE (thrusting his head out of the sack).   Oh, Scapino,
I can't bear it any longer.

SCAPINO.   Sir, my back is broken.

GERONTE.   How's that? It was my back that he beat.

SCAPINO.   Oh, no, no, it wasn't. That was my back he was
having a go at.

GERONTE.   What do you mean? I felt every single stroke and
I can feel every one of 'em still.

SCAPINO.   No, that was only the end of his . . . er, yardarm
that was reaching you.

GERONTE.   You should have moved off a bit then, and none
of it would have reached me.

SCAPINO.   Aagh! (Making GERONTE go back into the sack
again.) Don't look now, sir, get back in as quick as you
can. Just spotted another one. (Repeat same umbrella
business.) Just in time, just in time. It's a real vicious
Eastern type. Not a sound! Not a move, sir! (Long "spiel"
in stage Japanese a la Karate.) Pardon? *If you think I'm
going to repeat all that, you're a stupid idiot. Moment
please, there is something moving in the saki. I think I am
going to give gigantic Karate chop suey to saki.* No, sir,
please don't. Sir, that will be over my dead body. *If
necessary.* Please don't, sir. I've already been beaten up
once this morning already. *Then this is not your lucky day!
Con foo* . . . Ow! . . . *Ah so, etc.* (Short "spiel" and he
hits sack again, screaming in mock Karate.) *You, let that*

be a lesson to you, sonny Jim . . . Teach you not to be so insolent. Now I go, Chow . . . Mein. Oooh, may they take his guts for garters. (Falls on floor.)

GERONTE (popping his head out of the sack). Oh, I'm beaten to death.

SCAPINO. Oh, I'm killed.

GERONTE.   Why the devil must they keep hitting the sack?

SCAPINO.   I don't know, sir. I mean . . . the ushers just let them down the aisle. Sir, don't look 'round. I've just spotted another, sir. Get in as quick as you can. That's it, all the way to the bottom, and do not make a sound, whatever happens. (He goes to do umbrella business again but this time GERONTE pulls it in first.) Just in time, sir, just in time. It's a whole squad of English soldiers. (Asks audience to get ready to march.)

SCAPINO (as SQUAD).   I say, sergeant . . . *Yes, sir!* . . . I say, sergeant, have you seen that chappie Geronte anywhere? Hey what, what, what, what. *No, sir! He's not over here.* Sir, I say, there's his servant laddie over there with a sack. Let's investigate. (To audience.) *Company by the left.* Quick. (Audience starts feet, making marching sounds.) *Wait for it . . .* (Hits someone on head who has started sound.) *By the left, march, left, right, left, right, left . . .* (To audience.) *Keep up in the back there. Left . . . right . . . left . . . right, left. Brass bands . . . forward.* (Puts sausage to lips, imitates brass band marching and playing theme from "The Bridge on the River Kwai.") Then, I say there, chappie, can you tell us where we can find Signor Geronte; hey, what, what, what, what, tallyho what.

SCAPINO.   Sir, look, I swear I do not know where he is. You're the third lot of people that have looked for him today.

SCAPINO (as SQUAD).   Now, look, chappie, either you tell
us where he is or we shall attack your sack. (Sack falls
over; GERONTE has fainted.)

SCAPINO.   Sir, sir, for the last time, sir, I do not know where
he is.

SCAPINO (as SQUAD).   Right, then. Sergeant, bring up the
cavalry. Right! Cavalry—Forward. (Imitates cavalry;
stomping and neighing of horses.) I say, sergeant! Yes, sir?
Keep those damn horses quiet. (Then orders.)
Horses—Quiet! Now for the last time, are you going to tell
us where we can find Signor Geronte?

SCAPINO.   Sir, look, for the last time, I swear I don't know.

SCAPINO (as SQUAD).   Right then, sergeant, prepare to
charge. (GERONTE pokes head out of sack and sees
SCAPINO acting as SQUAD.) *Yes, sir!* Artillery, brass
band, platoon, my lords, ladies and gentlemen, prepare to
charge . . . Charge! (Just as he is going to turn around and
beat the sack, he sees GERONTE, who has come out of
the sack. They stare at each other, then SCAPINO runs off,
out the upstage exit. GERONTE can't catch him because
the sack is around his legs.)

GERONTE.   The traitor. The villain. The scoundrel. (He
kicks sack and strains his leg and back.) I'll make you pay
for this.

(ZERBINETTA enters.)

ZERBINETTA (laughing, not seeing GERONTE).   Oh, I'll
die of laughing. Ha, ha, ha, ha. It's too funny. (Sits.
Laughs.) What a fool the old fellow was. (Laughs.)

GERONTE.   It's not funny. You've no business to laugh at it.

ZERBINETTA.   What did you say, signor?

GERONTE.   I said you've no right to make fun of me.

ZERBINETTA.   Of you?

GERONTE. Yes.

ZERBINETTA. Why, who intends to make fun of you?

GERONTE.   You come here to laugh at me to my face?

ZERBINETTA. It's nothing to do with you, I was laughing to
myself at a story I've just heard. The funniest ever.
(Laughs.) It's about a trick . . . (Sits in upstage right chair
at right table.) . . . that was played by a son on his father
to cheat him of his money.

GERONTE.   By a son on his father to cheat him of his money?

ZERBINETTA. Yes. And you wouldn't have to press me very
hard for me to tell you the whole story. I'm bursting to tell it
to someone.

GERONTE.   Then let me press you; tell me it.

ZERBINETTA (slamming GERONTE into chair).   Oh,
thank you. I'll be delighted . . . (She prods him.) . . . My
young man is in the condition of many a suitor. . . .
Money is the least of his attributes. He has a father who,
though he is rich, is the meanest of misers. Now what was
his name? Um . . . (She prods him.) . . . perhaps you can
help me. Think of someone in this city who is known as the
greediest, meanest, nastiest of all . . .

GERONTE.   I wouldn't know him.

ZERBINETTA.   There is an "onte" in his name.

GERONTE.   "Onte."

ZERBINETTA.   "Orante."

GERONTE.   "Oronte."

ZERBINETTA.   "Organte."

GERONTE.   "Argante."

ZERBINETTA.   No, no, no . . . Ber . . . Beronte.

GERONTE.   Emily Bronte?

ZERBINETTA.   Geronte! (She hits him.) That's the one.
That's the name. He's the meanest man in Naples! (She hits
him. GERONTE crosses and sits on bench.) The gypsies
had decided to leave town today and my young man was

going to lose me for want of money when he was relieved
        by the genius of his servant who got it out of the miser. As
        for the servant's name, I'll never forget it—it is Scapino.
GERONTE (aside). Hah! The sniveling cockroach.
ZERBINETTA. This is how he tricked . . . (Takes his
        umbrella.) . . . the old fool. Ha, ha. Ha, ha. The thought
        of it has started me off again. Ha, ha, ha.
GERONTE. Go on, go on.
ZERBINETTA. He seeks out this Geronte, ha, ha, ha, and
        tells him that walking on the quayside with the son, they
        were invited aboard a boat by a friendly Turk. Ha, ha, ha.
GERONTE. I hate Turks.
ZERBINETTA. Ha, ha. Whilst they were eating and drinking,
        the boat put to sea, and the Turk sent poor Scapino by skiff
        to tell the old miser that his son would be carried off to
        Algiers if he did not pay an immediate ransom of five
        hundred thousand lire. The old man just couldn't bring
        himself to pay the money, so he tried a hundred ridiculous
        ways of getting out of it. After many windings and turnings,
        sighs and groans, "What the devil was he doing on board
        that boat." Ha, ha, ha, ha. But as I said, in the end our
        Scapino triumphed . . . but you're not laughing. Don't you
        think it's funny?
GERONTE (taking back umbrella). The young man's a
        scoundrel, an insolent blockhead, and he shall be punished
        by his father for the trick he's played. The gypsy is an
        inconsiderate, impertinent hussy to laugh at a man of honor.
        I'll teach her to come here debauching people's children.
        And the *valet* is a *villain* who'll be *sent* to *prison* before
        tomorrow morning. I hate gypsies. (He exits.)

(SYLVESTRO enters from cafe.)

SYLVESTRO. Hey . . . did you realize that the old fellow
        you were talking to is your young man's father?

Part Two — scapino!

ZERBINETTA.   I was just beginning to have my suspicions; I
    told him his own story before I realized it.
SYLVESTRO.   What, his own story?
ZERBINETTA.   Yes. I was bursting to tell it to someone. Oh
    . . . (An Italian expletive.) . . . what does it matter?
    Things can't get any worse for us.
SYLVESTRO.   Your tongue must be long enough for two.
    You can't even keep your own secrets.
ZERBINETTA.   Oh, yaaaahhh! (Sticks tongue out at him.)

(ARGANTE enters.)

ARGANTE.   Hey there, Sylvestro.
SYLVESTRO.   Get inside. There's my master calling me.
    (ZERBINETTA exits into cafe.)
ARGANTE (coming to bench).   So, you and that other rascal
    Scapino have conspired together to cheat me, and my son's
    in it, too. Do you think I'm going to stand for it?
SYLVESTRO.   Yes!
BOTH.   No!

(GERONTE enters.)

SYLVESTRO.   Now, really, sir. If that scoundrel, Scapino, has
    played you some trick or other, I wash my hands of the
    whole affair.
ARGANTE.   I'm not going to let myself be made a fool of.
SYLVESTRO.   Yes . . . er . . . No! (Exits to cafe.
    GERONTE sits on end of bench; other end goes up.)
GERONTE.   Ah, Signor Argante, you see me weighed down
    by misfortune. (ARGANTE sits on other end, and bench
    levels.)
ARGANTE.   You see me, too, Signor Geronte, in the slough of
    despond.

GERONTE.   That criminal Scapino has tricked me out of five
    hundred thousand lire.
ARGANTE.   And that self-same criminal Scapino has cheated
    me, too, of two hundred thousand lire.
GERONTE.   Not only did he trick me out of five hundred
    thousand lire, he's treated me in a way which I'm too
    ashamed to explain! But I'll pay him back for it.
ARGANTE.   I'll make sure he pays for the tricks he's played
    on us.

(SYLVESTRO has appeared on the cafe balcony.)

SYLVESTRO (aside).   Please, God, don't let them find out I
    was mixed up in all this.
GERONTE.   But this isn't the end of the story, Signor
    Argante. One misfortune follows another . . . the daughter
    I expected to arrive today is lost. She and her mother set
    out some time ago from Marseilles and are reported to have
    been lost in the ship they sailed in.

(NURSE enters from cafe.)

ARGANTE.   Why, oh, why, did you not bring her here with
    you?
GERONTE.   Reasons, reasons! Business and family interests
    forced me to keep this second marriage a great secret.
NURSE.   Oh, Signor Pandolfo!
GERONTE (standing).   You here, nurse?
NURSE (falling on her knees).   Oh, Signor Pandolfo . . .
GERONTE (opening umbrella to block ARGANTE's
    vision).   Don't call me Pandolfo here. Call me Geronte.
    The reasons which forced me to take another name at
    Marseilles exist no longer.
NURSE.   Alas, what troubles this change of name has caused
    us in trying to find you here.

GERONTE.   Us? Then where are my daughter and her
   mother?

NURSE.   Your daughter, signor, is close by. But before you see
   her, I must beg you to forgive us, for we were penniless and
   starving and thought we should never see you again. I must
   beg you to forgive me for having let her be married.
   (ARGANTE stands, crosses to them.)

GERONTE.   My daughter married?

NURSE.   Yes, sir.

GERONTE.   To whom?

NURSE.   To a young gentlemen called Ottavio, son of a
   certain Signor Argante.

GERONTE.   Good God!

ARGANTE.   What a coincidence!

GERONTE (starting downstage).   Show us, show us quickly
   where she is.

NURSE.   Follow me into that house over there. (NURSE,
   ARGANTE and GERONTE exit.)

SYLVESTRO (on balcony).   Well. I'd never believe it if I
   hadn't seen it with my own ears . . .

(SCAPINO enters balcony.)

SCAPINO.   Well, Sylvestro, how's tricks?

SYLVESTRO.   I've got two little bits of information for you.
   One's a surprise. Ottavio's worries are over. Our Giacinta
   turns out to be none other than Signor Geronte's daughter.
   Luck's brought about the very thing the fathers most
   intended. The other bit of information, no surprise, is that
   both the fathers are full of terrifying threats about your
   future, especially Signor Geronte.

SCAPINO.   Well, threats never did anyone harm, did they?
   They're clouds passing by, high in the sky. (Spoken like
   poetry.)

SYLVESTRO.   Yes, well, just you watch out. I wouldn't put it

past those two boys to make it up with their fathers, and
then where would you be, eh?

SCAPINO.   Yes, well, just you leave that to me.

SYLVESTRO.   Hey, hide yourself. Here they come.

   (SCAPINO exits.)

(Enter GERONTE, ARGANTE, NURSE and GIACINTA.)

GERONTE.   Come along, my dear. Come home with me. My
happiness would have been complete if only I'd been able to
see your mother with you.

ARGANTE.   Here comes Ottavio, right on cue.

(OTTAVIO enters from cafe. SYLVESTRO exits balcony.)

ARGANTE.   Come, son, come celebrate with us the happy
occasion of your marriage.

OTTAVIO (who has not seen GIACINTA).   No, Father, all
your plans of marriage mean nothing to me. I must be plain
with you; you have heard of the secret marriage I made.

ARGANTE. Yes, but you don't know . . .

(SYLVESTRO enters from cafe.)

OTTAVIO.   I know all I need to know.

ARGANTE.   I must tell you about Signor Geronte's daughter.

OTTAVIO.   Signor Geronte's daughter means nothing to me.

GERONTE.   But she's the one . . .

OTTAVIO.   No, sir, I will not be shaken.

SYLVESTRO.   Just let him get a . . .

OTTAVIO.   Shut up, you. I don't want to hear.

ARGANTE.   Your wife . . .

OTTAVIO.   No, Father, I'll die rather than desert my lovely
Giacinta. (Crossing to her.) This is the girl to whom I'm

married; I'll love her all my life and never even look at
another woman.

ARGANTE.   But she's the one we want you to have. Oh, my
God. What an idiot he is. Never listens to anyone but
himself.

(Enter ZERBINETTA from cafe.)

GIACINTA.   It's true, Ottavio. This is the father I have lost.
All our troubles are over. *Zerbinetta!* (Going to her.)
Father, please don't let me be separated from this dear
friend; if you knew her you would love her as much as I do.
(All move upstage.)

GERONTE.   You want me to allow a creature who's ensnared
your brother into my house, a creature who threw a
thousand insults in my face not half an hour ago?

ZERBINETTA.   Sir, forgive me. I should never have spoken in
that way if I'd known it was you, and then I only knew you
by repute.

GERONTE.   What do you mean, "repute?"

ZERBINETTA.   As the meanest, most greediest . . .
(GERONTE goes for her. She moves away.)

GIACINTA.   Father, my brother's love for her is deep and
true, and I'll answer for her virtue. (OTTAVIO moves to
her.)

GERONTE.   That's all very well. Would you have me marry
my son to her? A girl of the streets, that nobody knows?

(LEANDRO enters.)

LEANDRO.   Father!

GERONTE.   Yes.

LEANDRO.   You need no longer complain that I love a girl
without a name or fortune. The gypsies who sold her to me
revealed she was born in this city . . .

OTHERS.   City?

LEANDRO.   And to a well-known family . . .

OTHERS.   Family!

LEANDRO.   They stole her away when she was four years old.

OTHERS.   Four!

LEANDRO (going to ZERBINETTA).   And here is a
    bracelet that may reveal to us . . . that may reveal to us
    exactly who her real parents are. (Takes off her bracelet;
    holds it in air.)

ARGANTE (reaching over, taking bracelet with cane).
    Unbelievable! This bracelet proves she's my very own
    daughter whom I lost at the age you spoke of.

GERONTE.   *Your* daughter?

ARGANTE.   Yes, indeed. And now I look closely I see in her
    face all our family features.

ZERBINETTA.   Father! (She embraces ARGANTE.)

GIACINTA.   Goodness me, what an extraordinary
    coincidence!

(CARLO enters. All begin to move upstage as HEADWAITER
    and WAITER 2 bring table from cafe and set it at center
    and LEANDRO and OTTAVIO position bench in front of
    table.)

CARLO.   Signores, there has been a terrible accidente.

ALL.   Accidente?

CARLO.   Poor Scapino!

ALL.   Scapino?

GERONTE.   I will see that wretch hanged.

CARLO.   Oh, sir, you won't have to worry yourself about that.
    As he was passing by the scaffolding of a new building a
    stone-cutter's hammer fell on his head. . . .

(WAITER 1 starts down left aisle carrying SCAPINO over his
    shoulder.)

ALL.   Oh!

CARLO.   . . . fractured his skull . . .

ALL.   Oh!

CARLO.   . . . and scattered his brains up . . . (Points.) . . .
    and down . . . (Points.) . . . the street.

ALL.   Ugh!

CARLO.   He's dying and his last wish is to be brought here to
    say a few last words to you all.

ARGANTE.   Where is he?

CARLO.   Here he comes now.

(Enter SCAPINO carried by WAITER 1. His head is
bandaged.)

ALL.   Oh! . . . (SCAPINO moans.) Oh! . . . (SCAPINO
    moans.) Oh! . . . (WAITER places him on table.)

SCAPINO (groaning).   Ooooh, oooh. Signores, signores, you
    see me now . . . you see me in this tragic state. (Moans.)

ALL.   Oh.

SCAPINO.   Signores . . . Before I die I had to come to beg
    forgiveness of all those that I've ever offended. (Moans.)

ALL.   Ooooh!

SCAPINO.   Yes, signores, before I breathe my last breath I beg
    you from the bottom of your hearts to forgive me
    everything I've ever done. . . .

ALL.   Si, si . . .

SCAPINO.   . . . especially Signor Argante and Signor Geronte
    . . .

ARGANTE.   For my part, Scapino, I forgive you.

ALL.   Bravo.

ARGANTE.   Go and die in peace.

SCAPINO (to GERONTE).   But it's you, Signor Geronte,
    that I have offended most with that cruel beating I gave you
    earlier . . .

GERONTE.   Don't exhaust yourself. I forgive you as well.

SCAPINO.   But it was a horrible cheek of me to give you that
    good hiding in the sack . . .
ALL.   Hiding . . . sack . . . etc.
GERONTE.   Let's forget it.
SCAPINO.   Now that I am dying, sir, I can't express my
    sorrow enough for that sausage trick I played on . . .
ALL.   Sausage?
GERONTE.   Oh, God, shut up!
SCAPINO.   The sausage trick when he was in the sack . . .
GERONTE.   *Shut up*. I tell you. I've forgiven you everything.
SCAPINO.   Oh, what joy, sir. Do you really forgive me from
    the bottom of your heart the uh . . . pretty polly . . .
    (ALL laugh.)
GERONTE.   Yes, yes, yes, I forgive you everything.
SCAPINO.   Sir, I can't tell you how much better I feel for
    those few kind words.
GERONTE.   Quite. But I forgive you only on one condition.
SCAPINO.   What?
GERONTE.   That you die. If you recover, I take it all back.
ALL.   Oooooh!
SCAPINO (more groans).   Ooooh, oooh, sir, I'm sinking fast
    . . . I'm feeling weaker every moment.
ARGANTE.   Signor Geronte, to celebrate our happiness, I beg
    you to forgive him unconditionally.
ALL (running to audience).   Si, si . . . Forgive him, forgive
    . . . forgive him. . . .
GERONTE (screaming).   Basta! Basta! (To ACTORS and
    audience.) Shall I forgive him?
ALL.   Yes!
GERONTE.   . . . No!
ALL.   Yes!
GERONTE.   . . . No!
ALL.   Yes! (GERONTE raises his hand. There is silence.)
GERONTE.   All right, I forgive him.
ALL.   Hooray! (Shouts and applause. EVERYONE runs for

glasses, sings and dances fast version of "Minestrone Macaroni.")

Pollo All Americana,
Scampi Fritti In Brodo
Vermichelli
Talliachelli
Capuchino Espresso.

Minestrone Macaroni,
Ravioli Aux Crevette,
Caramella In Padella,
Avocado Vinaigrette.

Scallopina Valdostana,
Bistecca Con Risotto,
Vermichelli
Talliachelli
Da Un Buon Appetito.

Minestrone Macaroni
Ravioli Aux Crevette
Caramella In Padella
Avocado Vinaigrette.

(Once through; then repeat first two verses; toast, drink and throw glasses. At end of song they throw plastic glasses to audience and do slow instrumental humming song as they exit audience aisles. SCAPINO exits last, cafe.)

GROUP curtain call.

SCAPINO curtain call. SCAPINO calls all on stage. They come out and sit. WAITER 2 brings SCAPINO his guitar. SCAPINO talks to audience.

SCAPINO.   Ladies and gentlemen . . . wait a minute . . .
we're not finished yet. I'll tell you why—we're not going
home yet because there is one song in this show that we
have been singing from the word go. It goes like this.
(Hums "Minestrone Macaroni" melody.) We were singing
it at the very end. Now as I was looking out, all of you were
smiling . . . all of you . . . and then we got to the musical
instruments and all of it changed . . . it changed to "what a
bunch of idiots," so tonight we are going to split the
audience right down the center . . . so . . . you, sir . . .
you . . . he's grinning away . . . cross your legs or move to
the right . . . we will have . . . (To CAST.) . . . what do
you want . . . (Trombones, mandolins.) . . . right . . .
(To audience.) . . . this side trombones, this mandolins
. . . no, really, you can get the most romantic sound . . .
all you have to do is make sure you spit directly on the neck
of the person in front of you . . . right then . . . in the
back . . . (Pointing to GERONTE, ARGANTE,
NURSE.) . . . the old dears, the cellos . . . (NURSE
spreads her legs. Laughs. SCAPINO turns to her.) . . . put
it down . . . right, then . . . this side trombones . . . this
side mandolins . . . all the adults be kids again . . . it's a
marvelous feeling, I promise you . . . (Starts to play.) . . .
Wait a minute . . . ladies and gentlemen, I would like to
bring to your attention that in our audience tonight there
are three people who are not enjoying themselves one bit
. . . I mean it. There are three people among you who are
hating every minute of this . . . we got little peepholes in
the set and we watch you all night long . . . now those
three people wherever you are, we know exactly where you
are sitting . . . that's all right, though, we know some
people don't like clowning about . . . that's all right . . .
you sit back and relax, we'll make idiots of ourselves . . .
then we'll stop . . . point to you . . . and you'll stand up
and do it on your own . . . right, then . . . here we go.

ALL mime instruments and hum together as CAST goes among audience and then exits.

Final curtain calls.

Then WAITRESS comes out and kicks jukebox for the last time and it plays.

END OF PLAY